D042225Ɛ

*f*P

ALSO BY KATIE ROIPHE

The Violet Hour
In Praise of Messy Lives
Uncommon Arrangements
Still She Haunts Me
Last Night in Paradise
The Morning After

THE
POWER
NOTEBOOKS

*

KATIE
ROIPHE

FREE PRESS

NEW YORK   LONDON   TORONTO   SYDNEY   NEW DELHI

Free Press
An imprint of Simon & Schuster, Inc.
1230 Avenue of the Americas
New York, NY 10020

First Free Press hardcover edition March 2020

FREE PRESS and colophon are trademarks of Simon & Schuster, Inc.

Interior Illustrations by Katy Hunchar
Grateful acknowledgment is made to:
Alfred A. Knopf for permission to quote an excerpt from "Bicenntenial," copyright © 2014 by Dan Chaisson.
The Art Shay estate for permission to print the Simone de Beauvoir photograph.

For information about special discounts for bulk purchases, please contact Simon & Schuster Special Sales at 1-866-506-1949 or business@simonandschuster.com.

The Simon & Schuster Speakers Bureau can bring authors to your live event. For more information or to book an event contact the Simon & Schuster Speakers Bureau at 1-866-248-3049 or visit our website at www.simonspeakers.com.

Interior design by Carly Loman

Manufactured in the United States of America

10 9 8 7 6 5 4 3 2 1

Library of Congress Cataloging-in-Publication Data is available.

ISBN 978-1-9821-2801-2
ISBN 978-1-9821-2803-6 (ebook)

Women in power are seen as breaking down barriers, or alternatively as taking something to which they are not quite entitled.

—MARY BEARD

I read Doris Lessing in literature class and that depressed the shit out of me too. I just hated reading work by women or about women because it always added up the same. Loss of self, endless self-abnegation, even as the female was trying to be an artist, she wound up pregnant, desperate, waiting on some man.

—EILEEN MYLES

SIMONE DE BEAUVOIR, CIRCA 1950

For Tim

AUTHOR'S NOTE

Please note that when I use the word "power" in these pages I don't mean geopolitical power, or socioeconomic power or electoral power, or power in the broad Foucauldian sense. This is not a book about the vast inequalities and violence of the world we live in. It focuses on little things: the dynamics between people (friends, strangers, intimates) in a room. These dynamics reflect larger power relations, to be sure, but those are not my subject here.

In addition, please note that I have, in places, entirely altered or tinkered with names and/or identifying details of people referred to in these pages.

I began these notebooks in a time of upheaval a little over two years ago. They feel like nothing else I have ever written.

My usual ways of being in the world were no longer working. My theories and interpretations were wrong or inadequate. In other words: one of those rare, disconcerting moments of openness we are sometimes forced into.

In my published writing, I took stands. I made arguments. But in the very early morning, before anyone was awake, I was working on these notebooks. Here I wasn't arguing anything. Here I was circling, contradicting myself. Here I was keeping a secret record of the uncertainties, doubts, shifts.

I had been writing about women and power all of my adult life, maybe even before my adult life. A not-entirely-friendly review said one of my books was "infused with what has long obsessed her: the power dynamics of sex and love." My whole life I had been making arguments about those dynamics, and my positions were roughly consistent, but my own experience with power was oddly untouched by these arguments. I had never gotten close to that experience.

The thing that I kept coming back to in these notebooks, the thing that was getting me out of bed before dawn, lay hidden under the particulars of my work life or love life or life as a mother, which are no more or less interesting than anyone else's. These particulars seemed to suggest more ambivalence, more ambiguity, more fear surrounding the issue of power than my published writing acknowledged. So in darkness, for myself, I tried to work on the problem.

In these early mornings, I found myself revisiting scenes from my life and the lives of women I knew, even if I didn't quite know why. I recorded stray observations, unresolved obsessions, passages from books I was reading. I excavated notebooks from my teenage years because the problem of power had been with me even then.

I recognized in myself an unseemly will to power, a possibly unnatural fascination with it, an aspiration toward it. But I also saw myself, at times, failing to hang on to a decent amount of it. I saw myself sometimes wanting to give it up or get rid of it or hide it in surprising ways.

It sometimes seemed to me that we like the idea of powerful women, but we don't like powerful women themselves. I wanted to get at the hidden ways that we internalize that contempt. The ways we deflect competitiveness or resentment, but they are hard to measure or document.

In my regular life, I wrote books about writers' lives (and loves and deaths) that took years of research. While I was working on these books, I spent long afternoons poring through letters and diaries. I was looking for something that could help me, but this work was too slow and meticulous for what I needed now.

Instead, I obsessed over writers whose lives seemed to hold out some sort of template even if it upended certain expectations I had for successful women. Why did Mary McCarthy have to ask her husband for a nickel to make a telephone call? Why did Sylvia Plath fall in love with, as she put it, the only man who could boss her around? Why did Edith Wharton, at the height of her success, write to her faithless lover, "I don't want to win—I want to lose everything to you!"? I collected the details here in the hope that they would help me later.

Here is a subject that I kept coming back to: women strong in public, weak in private. Is there a particular kind of abjection that some of us are drawn to, participate in, possibly romanticize, even though nothing about our external lives necessarily suggests it? If so, is there a way out of it? In the notebooks the questions multiplied. How to be someone who has to win every argument with a man and also sometimes likes the idea of being overpowered. How to build a whole world inside the contradictions.

The notebooks required me to do things I otherwise never let myself do: admit weakness, give up control, acknowledge doubt, have no idea where I am going.

In these pages, I often had the feeling of being at sea or overwhelmed. In normal life, I rush to resolution. I organize my thoughts. I make points. I care about being right. But with the notebooks, it felt like I was laying out pieces of a puzzle. Or like I was taking notes for some later time when I would see the patterns, when the arc would announce itself, the messages become clear.

There is in the notebooks confusion, self-contempt, conflict, which is not always fun to write through. While I was working on them, I often thought of abandoning them. But I craved a kind of wandering not available to me in the increasingly rigid forms of my life, the articles I wrote, the authority of the classroom, the routines of motherhood. I wanted a way out of my usual way of looking at things.

I was working on something I didn't understand—containing, experimenting, following possibly disturbing tangents, pursuing diverging lines of thought, gathering in one place.

Here's a thumbnail of my life during the years covered in the notebooks: In my early thirties, I got married to H., and a year later we had a baby girl. By the time she was two and a half, the marriage had fallen apart, and I was single again. After that, I had an entanglement with a much younger man that lasted about a year and a half, and got pregnant by accident. He left and moved to London, so I was on my own again, with a newborn boy. I now had two children with two different fathers, neither of whom I was with. After five years, during which I lived alone with the children, I met Tim. During this time, I got my first job, taught for twelve years, wrote four books, dozens of articles.

Birth

The baby's father slept over the night before he was born. The fact that we had broken up seemed less important than having a man in my bed the night before the birth. The forms were important to me.

I was awake for hours staring at the tin ceiling while D. slept, three days' stubble, a coin with a saint on it dangling from a chain around his neck. After months of not speaking, an ambiguous space had opened up between us, a careful prickly civility.

His Englishness, meanwhile, could be a parody of itself. Even his more furious or simmering emails would end, "Hope it's not too cold there x" or "Hope you're surviving this rain x." There was really no situation too extreme or fraught for him to talk resourcefully about the weather. "I hate you," he might as well write, "I hope you are keeping warm in the snow x."

It may be there was a wisp of a fantasy that D. and I might somehow morph into a family. This fantasy was deranged, off, but I can't definitively say that it didn't exist. It felt at the time almost biologically impelled—like a family is de facto forming, and who are we to fight it?—but it may just have been cowardice or a complete shutdown of imagination on my part.

My instinct was camouflage, to assume the conventional patterns, to blend in, seek cover. The impulse was to secretly, stealthily develop a new life, to figure it out in private, protect it. It may not have helped that my uncharacteristic heft made me vulnerable, swampy; it made me feel like I was open to amorphous and imminent attack. Even taking the blue recycling bag of cans and milk cartons to the curb felt like a risk.

It's hard to explain the residual shame I felt, or if it's not precisely shame, it's some sort of shabby conventional sense of failure that I should have been able to rise above. I couldn't bear the idea of anyone looking down on us or feeling sorry for us or thinking that the baby's entrance into the world was somehow compromised or unfestive. I couldn't stand anyone thinking it was even a little bit sad that he would grow up without a father in our house, which is what basically everyone thought. I was alert to this even in people very close to me: an extra shade of warmth, a determination to make the best of a slightly diminished situation.

For some reason I couldn't summon the independence or fearlessness I had talked or cajoled myself into earlier. I reverted to a more conventional pregnant person, a nursery decorator, a woman who goes to Ikea and buys a cherry red lamp. I couldn't muster the boldness or the not caring what people think that I usually try for. It was like in my new, giant, less nimble state, I couldn't get around the idea that there is a way you are supposed to have a baby, and this was not that way.

Of course, being alone is more fun when you are not hugely pregnant. Six months earlier, not visibly pregnant, I was with a writer who was doing research at a strip club in Queens, with a vodka tonic in front of me, on a shady sort of date. The room I slept in that night was generic and hotelish, a giant mirror propped up next to the bed and an insanely comfortable fluffy white duvet. I woke up at dawn, purples and yellows streaking the sky above navy water towers and rooftops, half reveling in, half horrified by the incongruousness. Mostly the more flagrant departures, the unlikely adventuring, still cheered me up and egged me on. What not to expect when you are expecting.

That freezing morning, grabbing a milky coffee on the way home and ducking into the subway on Houston Street was the way I wanted to feel all the time, this fullness, these signs of the continuing existence of my self, of abundance, or surprise. How long could I sustain it, though? In the back of my mind, I was afraid I was trading important things for the baby, trading my body itself, trading the prospect of a man in my house, as I put it to myself, since I could no longer picture anything as extreme or outlandish as marriage.

One frigid winter night I found myself having drinks and tomato soup at the Carlyle with an older woman I admire. She had a son on her own who was now in college. She said, matter-of-factly, "It'll probably be a year after the baby is born before you can even start thinking about going out with men." I was rattled. She can't mean a *year*.

One of my sisters offered to keep me company at the birth, but at the last minute I decided I'd better have the baby's father there, instead. I told myself it would make him understand that the baby was real and not an abstract, romantic concept for him to toss around to impress women over drinks, "I am a *father*." Or so I told myself. Really I was putting off the moment of being alone.

D. lived in far upstate New York, in a drafty, dark, woody house. It was monkish and fussy at the same time, if such a thing is possible, a piece of Indian block-print fabric draped over a white couch, a utilitarian layer of plastic wrap insulating the windows, a mattress on the floor under triangle eaves, the ambiance sort of Hemingway if Hemingway had taken women's studies classes. He had index cards full of notes pushpinned over the entire living room wall. He liked to map out his books on his walls, which struck me as a very male impulse, wanting your whole thought process made manifest, inflicting it on a room. The house was always very cold. He had a little silver drip coffee pot from Italy that made strong bitter coffee, and I would wake up very early and make myself some.

We had in common all the things I never had in common with my husband. We talked about the books I never talked about in my marriage. One night we spent three hours talking about John Berryman's *Dream Songs* and the poets who had visited Ezra Pound in the mental hospital, St. Elizabeth's.

D. is so skinny it is hard to believe that he is not making some sort of statement with his skinniness. I found it unnerving to sleep with someone who is almost smaller than me. It's like sleeping with a sparrow.

A couple of times, I drove up to visit him in a generic white rental car. I thought of it as the "witness protection car" because it felt like we were assuming new identities, fleeing vicious and irrational enemies. We were on the run. One day we almost lost the white car in the Target parking lot. We wandered the rows of cars looking for this car that wasn't ours.

At six in the morning, we took a taxi to the hospital. In the operating room, D. wore blue scrubs, which make anyone look like a good person. The baby cried before they lifted him out, which the doctors seemed to think was an auspicious sign. When they handed him to me, he was very calm.

Meanwhile, D., in his hospital shower cap, had his hand on my head; we were pretending, we were passing. The prospect of explaining to every nurse and doctor that we were not together and he was about to move to London—that though it seems like he is around, he is not, in fact, around—seemed too exhausting in my post-partum state, and possibly any state.

He was, however, very polite and helpful in a hospital setting, getting me a ginger ale, checking on the baby, who was in one of those French-fry warmers. He was wearing a bright yellow flowered button-down shirt. Otherwise, he had divested himself of any personality and was what might, if I had been more alert or attuned, have seemed ominously brisk and vacant. Secretly I thought: like a valet.

At first Violet, my six-year-old, didn't believe D. was the father. She had met him when she was three, climbing up the three flights to his walk-up in a princess dress. Her exact words were "But he's not a kid person!" Later, she said, "You have no proof he's the father."

In the hospital, though, the farce of what we were doing, which could have been depressing, seemed worth it, the sham enfolded and swaddled in hospital routine. The fact that he was being faux helpful or faux there was not relevant or interesting in the context of the maternity ward, with its little dignitaries wheeled around in clear plastic carts. The sign on mine read "Baby Boy Roiphe."

I was wearing a nightgown with puffy sleeves. I had dark plum circles under my eyes and hair like straw. The Percocet created cloud cover in my brain.

My father brought my mother tiny roses when I was born, and I was aware of not having those roses, not feeling the crinkle of cellophane, not putting them into one of those plastic hospital pitchers next to my bed. This is not the tiny roses way to have a baby.

I fill out the birth certificate with my name as the only parent. The feeling is of taking a test that I am doing very badly on even though I studied. I am also getting the sense that the nurse who is assisting me feels sorry for us. There are husbands holding doors open for berobed wives, holding smoothies, holding metallic balloons with pink bears on them, milling around the common area where we are doing the paperwork. "Just go ahead and leave that line blank," the nurse says encouragingly. It seems as if she is pretending nothing is wrong, when she feels like something is wrong. "Take care of yourself, honey," she says when I hand her back the pen. Does she say that to everyone or only the one-name-on-the-birth-certificate people?

When D.'s mentor, a Shakespeare professor, learned that I was having the baby, he said, "I suppose it will be fine, unless something happens to Katie."

When I left the hospital a nurse warned me that I wouldn't be able to carry the baby up the stairs in my house myself, but of course when

I got home I carried the baby up the stairs myself. It turns out the hospital's list of rules for post-caesarian care is not for the husbandless or partnerless, but it also turns out nothing happens to you if you ignore it.

When the baby was eight days old, I took him to a July Fourth barbecue thrown by my English next-door neighbors. There were hot dogs and hamburgers and mustardy potato salad and a pink flowering camellia tree and blond children and coolers of beer in melting ice. There were European couples, men with blue eyes and accents, women with blond choppy haircuts and clogs. Someone broke a bottle. Afterward, when I was back in my bedroom, the baby asleep on sheets festooned with serious-looking animals standing up playing trumpets in his wicker bassinet next to my bed, it was like being suddenly tumbled by a wave: I am alone.

Nearly three years later, on the bus, I turned to the baby, who was by then of course a boy, and asked, "Are you going to be scared if we go to the planetarium?" The last time we went, he was terrified by the big bang, which was, to be fair, nearly as loud as the real big bang. He considered. "In my brain I will not be afraid, but in my heart I will be afraid."

Catastrophe

Françoise Gilot talking to a friend at the beginning of her relationship with Picasso:

"'You're headed for a catastrophe,' she said. I told her she was probably right but I felt it was the kind of catastrophe I didn't want to avoid."

The Car

My husband and I step into the thirty-year-old sky blue diesel Mercedes. When the engine starts, it shakes and vibrates, you can feel every ounce of gas as it moves through the car; this car is, in fact, as close as you can come to a horse and carriage in the modern world. But we can't start the car yet. We've stayed too long at our friends' house. The baby is perilously tired. I was aware of her getting tired as it was happening, but I liked sitting with my friends on the picnic bench in their overgrown garden, drinking wine as the babies played, and hadn't wanted to leave. Now the baby struggles in an impressive display of civil disobedience. The baby will not under any circumstances submit to the car seat. I try to bend her as she arches her back, but as I feel H. getting angrier, I am getting more rattled and the baby is getting slipperier. "Come on," I plead. "Daddy needs to start the car." I know it is a mistake to show weakness to the baby. She will never get into the car seat now. Finally I manage to strap her in, but she can't accept the blow to her dignity. The baby howls.

H. is very tall, with black hair, sunglasses with clear frames, green lenses, three, actually four, different colors of seersucker suits hanging in his closet. He says, icy calm, "Why can't you control her?" He drives, the baby wails. The car coughs and rattles. I think he may hit another car as he swerves lanes. Then he stops, the brakes shrieking impressively. "Get out." I wait. He says again, "Get out." I take the baby, who is amazed into silence. I have no stroller. I have no money. The air is fresh and violet. It is dusk on one of those long blank blocks near the projects, the stretch of warehouses and taxi yards. I carry the baby. The baby becomes quite cheerful, perceiving a holiday atmosphere. The baby has probably never witnessed such an effective display of her own power. I walk over a mile carrying the baby in my arms. When we pass brownstones, I glimpse the parlors through the long windows, gold orbs hanging from ceilings, bits of molding like cake icing.

Later, when I tell the story to friends, they inevitably ask, "Why didn't you just say no?" *No, I won't get out of the car.* The question is so fantastical I don't even know how to answer. Why, they might as well wonder, didn't I step into a hovering spacecraft and take that all the way home?

We are and have for a long time been living in an apartment laced with tripwires. Will I put the knife down the wrong way on the dish rack, will I leave water in the teakettle, causing it to possibly rust, will I push the elevator button the wrong way? I know how crazy this sounds, but there is a wrong way to push the elevator button. If you don't push the "door closed" button at the same time as the "L" button, the door takes a surprisingly long time to close, which H. can't tolerate. I am aware that one small wrong move and the whole household will blow sky high; this awareness works its way into everything: I am never not being careful. This care I am taking, this elaborate many-frontiered vigilance, is exquisite but also never enough. I will always fail. This knowledge oppresses and liberates me a little until I am almost relieved when I make a mistake. It's done.

Did I do it on purpose? I never quite know. I think of myself as intelligent and organized enough to keep up with his systems, his ways, but then I can't. My mind goes vague and dreamy at the crucial point. What normal person can't remember to leave the knife blade up on the drying rack?

Some of our neighbors call the building management to complain about the shouting. Our gruff eighty-six-year-old landlord calls to see if I am all right. When he calls, I feel like I have been caught at something, though I am not the one shouting.

My relation to the shouting is hard to explain. My response is not to react. I have made an art out of not reacting. I can not react to almost anything.

It is hard to reproduce the state I enter, quiet, still, vacating; it is almost active, the absence, vibrating. Like an animal running fast through a forest, nothing there but quivering leaves. This absence is probably frustrating to the angry man, to have nothing to bounce off of, to rail against, to be playing to an empty theater, to have no one tethering you to the earth. The anger is, among other things, a reaching out for someone, and to not react is, in a way, to abandon. The not reacting makes things worse.

I know this, but I can't help it. The shouting causes me to shut down, pack up, freeze. As if it is not happening if I don't react to it, as if I can walk away and preserve everyone's dignity. It is a wish, this not reacting, a wish that I could transport myself to another part of the planet where people are behaving better, a public place, at the very least, a calm coffee shop with stripped blond wood tables, where people talk in hushed voices over lattes with leaves drawn in the foam or stare silently at screens.

In a way, you could argue, the kind of absence I was cultivating is aggressive. Not caring or not appearing to care is, in its way, an assertion of power. Unruffled calm or even benumbed calm is its own kind of weapon; it is a declaration of moral superiority, a silent judgment, a showy and un-interrogated innocence, a way of putting oneself above or at least outside. You can see the angry man getting angrier when you don't react. To pretend it is not a provocation is a lie.

In these fights—the word "fights" is wrong, it implies discrete flare-ups, rather than a constant state—a little town with a school and a restaurant built on the side of a volcano would be more accurate—anyway, in these fights I am sometimes aware of anger as the appropriate response, but I don't feel anger. Mostly, I am afraid he will leave.

He, meanwhile—this is in the mostly predigital early aughts—is always glued to the news: papers, magazines, television news, the *New York Post*, the *New York Times*, *New York*, the *Wall Street Journal*, *The Economist*. At night he seems always to be sprawled, all six foot four of him, on our couch, spiraling deep into every level of news; no fire in the Bronx or teacher's strike on Long Island is too specific or local for him to follow minutely. It is as if he is collecting calamities and controversies, absorbing them into himself.

Sometimes I walk down the steps into the subway outside the lion's library where I am working and I hear a voice in my head: "Your husband doesn't like you." The voice is dispassionate, as if it comes from outside me, as if it were a natural resonance, as if I might somehow let myself slip into forgetting.

H. was the first man I was involved with who had an actual job. He got up in the morning, put on a suit and tie, and went into the office, which I found exotic and reassuring. He knew how to fix a car. He took me to New Delhi, where he had lived for a year and knew where to find the best *chana chaat* and how to call someone a "bad character" in Hindi. He was also the most beautiful man I knew, and I never became immune or even habituated to his looks. I kept all his letters—which were *not* writers' letters, not slick, not simultaneously written for another audience, an imaginary consumer of good prose—in a box. This all was still there.

One day the shouting is so bad that when I give the baby dinner in her high chair she can't eat because she is trembling. That's when I understand that he has to leave. It occurs to me that not a single friend of mine would recognize me if they were in the room.

The power he has over me feels physical. Although I am never consciously worrying about physical violence, the fear is still there when someone much larger and stronger than you is spiralingly out of control, furious. Behind the latent physical threat is another threat, which is that he will walk away. The power he has over me is how little I can imagine my life without him.

My parents had an unusually, implausibly happy marriage. Whatever else went wrong in our house, there was always the unshakable security of their relationship. This may be why divorce to me was unthinkable, unentertainable. It would be like my suddenly deciding to move to Prague and learn a new language and meet all new friends and raise the baby there. I was not able to face the failure of my will, my inability to stop or change or prevent what was happening. I was still, in my own way, trying to *do* something.

In the thick of it, I was writing a book on seven unusual marriages in Edwardian England. I channeled all my confusion and grief about my own marriage into intense research into the marriages of strangers who had died a long time before. I found it oddly comforting to read about distant, madly articulate people trying to sort through unmanageable romantic problems. "Where a man has been monstrous," I wrote, "the woman has almost always had some hand in creating her particular monster." I believed these words, was committed to them. But that was not how it felt. It felt like walking at night through a fairy-tale forest with giant navy leaves, and waking something terrible in a cave.

Here are some things I did that irritated him: being actually scared in a bad thunderstorm, taking too long to find my Metro card in my bag while trying to catch a subway, talking on the phone for ten minutes with a friend, reading a battered paperback of Graham Greene's *Travels with My Aunt*, sleeping.

I tried to think about this from his point of view. When you no longer love someone you are living with, signs of their continuing existence are annoying. You would prefer that they would cooperatively go out in a puff of smoke, and their stubborn refusal to do so can feel unfair.

Emily

My sister Emily once said to me, "There is no man anywhere so psychotic, so drunk, so helpless, so brutal, so indifferent, even just so annoying, that some woman somewhere isn't dying to take care of him."

Re-calculating

When they actually meet, my ex-husband reaches out to shake D.'s hand, and D. looks confused, as if the people on his planet, which he has fallen from like the Little Prince, do not shake hands.

D. and I are convalescing. I'm getting over my eight years with H. and the collapse of our marriage; D. is getting over a girlfriend he was with for a little while. What we both need is an old-fashioned sanatorium in the Alps with wicker chaise longues and nurses serving us iced tea and cold mountain air. What we have is each other.

There is a feeling between us that this affair doesn't count, that we are taking a little time off from our lives, which will, at some point in the fairly near future, resume. This feeling proves dangerous: many things happen while we are in the middle of this feeling, including the baby.

One of the other, more minor things that happens is that I learn to drive. Emily once told me that if I didn't learn to drive I would always be dependent on men and cities. "You'll get into a fight with a boyfriend at a 7-Eleven in the middle of nowhere, and he'll leave you there."

The first time I climb into the driver's seat of the generic white rental car, it feels like a spaceship. In the parking lot I have to remind myself which is the gas pedal and which is the brake.

During graduate school, while I was preparing for my general exams on all of English literature, I failed the written driving test twice, and this after studying the manual for many, many hours. In spite of having somehow obtained my license, I have never before driven on a highway. Sometimes I think about the trips I could have gone on, apple picking or reporting trips to the middle of nowhere, or how I could have driven on a trip to the archives in Los Angeles instead of taking the bus with the schizophrenics, but I can't. I watch my friends parallel park without panicking and feel excluded and wistful and trivially embittered, as if there is a rooftop club with a swimming pool and excellent cocktails that everyone else belongs to but that I will never join.

Over time this refusal of responsibility becomes more and more outlandish, more and more inconvenient, more and more an imposition on the people around you. You must be chauffeured, like a king, like a child.

This disability seems shameful, a secret indicator of other shameful things; an unreadiness for the world, a dependence so deep and unmanageable I will never rid myself of it, and yet I can't be sure that I want to.

By the time I reach my first on-ramp, I have developed an intense relationship with the early-version GPS, the giant old-fashioned square kind that suctions onto the windshield. The voice is bright, Australian, unflappable, exquisitely in control: "In two point three miles, turn left on Hayground Road."

Somewhere near Albany, it becomes clear to me that I could in no way drive without the voice. The voice gives the distinct impression

that there could not be a fire or accident or divorce anywhere around her. It is impossible to freak her out. If you miss your turn, she does not get hysterical. She says, with an endearing mechanical pause, "Re-calculating. Re-calculating."

It may be that I love the voice because it is the opposite of shouting. It may be that I like D. because he is the opposite of my husband.

I pull over at a gas station, and my back and arms ache because I have been clutching the wheel so tightly. It feels like I have special knowledge that I am not meant to drive, that my body will forget how to manage a car at the crucial moment. This skill I have now, this knowing how to drive, feels fragile, highly temporary, on loan.

Still, driving for hours on the highway, the trees floating past, feeling, finally, even a little bored (I am driving! And I am *bored*!), I feel an almost narcotic surge of accomplishment. I can't entirely believe it. It is as though someone has "let" me drive and probably shouldn't have. As if I have gotten away with something. But still, I am behind the wheel.

D. and I go for a swim in a lake and lie on a rock. We watch the horse races and bet on horses and drink vodka tonics out of red plastic cups. We grill swordfish on a tiny grill outside his house. We go to Target to buy plaid flannel sheets for his mattress on the floor.

In the city, I tell my friends this is a one-night stand that has somehow lasted a year and a half. When we see each other, it's always the last night on earth: there is too much wine, a frantic, addict-y ardor. It's never comfortable or calm or settled, not even for a couple of hours, and yet these nights string together and we are something to each other.

Coming back into the city, there was bumper-to-bumper traffic on the FDR. When it loosened, I was weaving in and out like a madman, like a driver! At the end, when I came to the rental place, the voice got confused because as I drove inside the garage, she thought I had overshot the address, so the last words I heard when they unplugged her were "Re-calculating. Re-calculating."

My choices during this time—starting, of course, with the choice to embark on a six-hour drive on the highway when you don't know which is the gas pedal and have a toddler who definitively needs you—seem questionable. I couldn't see how I was going to continue paying my rent, which my landlord raised precipitously at unpredictable moments. The voice seems to rescue me from all this. In two point three miles I can turn left.

Unfortunately, this drive did not free me or teach me. This brief phase was an exception, never to be reproduced.

People say to me, "But could you drive in an emergency?" They mean if your child had to get to the hospital or you had to flee the city for a terrorist event. I say yes, of course, which is what they want and expect me to say, but now, twelve years later, I am pretty sure it's a lie. In an emergency we die.

Stella

Once I wrote about betraying a close friend in college. I slept with a tall, handsome boy she had a tortured intermittent involvement with. I had loved her and hadn't cared at all about the boy, which made the whole episode particularly bewildering. In the book I changed her name to Stella. I changed identifying characteristics. It was meant to be a brutal examination of my destructive behavior when I was young. What I was thinking or not thinking in doing something so stupid. The act seemed so incomprehensible to the adult me that I wanted to re-create it for myself. The Stella in my head is smart, sarcastic, critical, daunting. When I tell the story, I have her ripping to shreds my theories and memories. She is the voice of common sense but also angry.

But back to the girl standing next to a tall boy by the water towers. The seconds before she leans into him or he leans into her. The sky a glowing navy blue. How would the girl herself have explained? I am afraid that she would have come out with something like "It felt like the right thing." (I can hear Stella launch into this one: "It felt like the right thing. Of course it felt like the right thing. But did you stop to think for one second in the midst of all this exalted feeling?") I am aware of how feeble this sounds, how predictable, how mundane, but I am trying to be as accurate as I can. In the moment, it felt like one of those exceptional situations that rises above conventional morality, "in the moment" being another one of those phrases one heard all the time back then. In the moment, one is not thinking; in the moment the physical takes precedence; this is, of course, the businessman's excuse with his secretary, the politician's excuse with his intern, the tired cliché, in fact, of every single adulterer with the gall and the paltriness of spirit to try to explain themselves, yet it is true: in the moment, it didn't feel as if there was a choice.

Suddenly at a reading in a bookstore, there she is in the audience. The real Stella. She is the not the college student in the piece. She is older, thinner, radiating anger.

I am terrified of her. Like the victim of a crime I have committed has come back to talk it over with me, but I am behind a podium and can't flee the scene.

I must have thought we would sleep together once and get it out of our systems. It turned out, however, that the boy believed in 'honesty,' an approach I would not have chosen on my own. He called Stella at the soonest possible second and told her. It was not hard to imagine the frantic look in Stella's eyes when he told her. Stella looked frantic when she had to pour cornflakes in a bowl. I hated him for telling her. I couldn't bear the idea of her knowing. Strangely enough, I felt protective of her, as if I could somehow protect her from the threat of myself.

I don't think I grasped right away the magnitude of what I had done. It felt like waking up in the middle of a Magritte painting and finding tiny men with bowler hats suddenly falling from the sky. It didn't make sense, even to me, and I was startled, in a way, to find that it was real. To have the boy in my house in

the morning wanting coffee, and to have his blue and green flannel shirt spread out on my floor, was for some reason extremely
startling. Cause and effect were sufficiently severed in my mind
that I had not apprehended the enormity of the betrayal. In the
light of day, it seemed a little unfair that I couldn't take it back.

Stella is standing on the line to sign books. When she reaches the
table, she says, "Don't you want to hear what I have to say?"

I manage to say yes I would. I get the sense that she would like to tell
me what she thinks in front of all of these people. Instead, I give her
my email so we can set up a time to talk. Of course, if she had written the story, it would be very different. The ways I represented the
situation would not feel accurate to her. I am afraid of her anger and
also my own obviously indefensible position. Whenever you represent
anyone, you are misrepresenting them: you will never capture them
exactly as they see themselves. To put your version on the page is an
act of supreme arrogance, of violence against what they know to be
true. You have taken or seized or twisted the meaning. You have stolen
the last word.

Her presence also rattles me because she isn't really Stella. The Stella
of the piece is a fantasy of her, the highly flawed projection of the
twenty-year-old I was or that twenty-year-old as I could best piece
her together in my guilty reminiscence. The conspicuous gap between
Stella and whoever this person is alarms me.

The next day I check my email constantly to see if she has written.
How will the conversation go? I can apologize even though the whole

essay is about learning that there are things you can't apologize for, that apologies themselves can turn into elaborate narcissistic performances, into self-justifications. She can enumerate the errors in the piece. She can tell me her version of what really happened. She can tell me that under the guise of eviscerating and repudiating my former self I am still somehow glorifying or romanticizing or obscuring a painful betrayal. She never emails.

I know there is something ruthless and unnatural about writing about your life in this way, about using or recycling it.

Gay Talese: "I'm detached always, with everyone. Now that I'm trying to write about my life with Nan, I realize the extent to which I've been an observer in a fifty-year marriage. I am always interested in the story that I could be writing if I were writing about what I'm doing. I could be swatting tennis balls, and I'm thinking of a scene on the tennis court. A case could be made that this is my main failing as a person. I am never there. Fully."

A chilling moment in the Joan Didion documentary:

> GRIFFIN DUNNE: What was it like to be a journalist in the room when you saw the little kid on acid?
> JOAN DIDION: Well it was . . . Let me tell you, it was gold. I mean, that's the long and the short of it is, you live for moments like that if you're doing a piece.

I don't think I would ever have had precisely that thought. But it's the same disease.

When my mother's autobiographical first novel, which included a damning portrait of her family and their milieu, came out in the sixties, her aunt bought out every single copy at her local bookstore so no one she knew would see it, and when the store restocked it, she bought them out again. My mother's publisher called her to happily report the book was a surprise bestseller in that one little neighborhood. My mother, like many writers of her generation, had the idea that she had to write "the truth." I don't have any idea that there is a "truth" or that I have to write anything at all. I can't claim any higher purpose that somehow justifies Stella's uneasiness about the story (I have a feeling Stella would point out that "uneasiness" is not a strong enough word here).

My students sometimes feel anxious when they decide to write personal essays. They worry about the feelings of the people they are writing about. Of course, they have chosen to write about themselves. They could have written about a remote topic instead but were somehow drawn to writing about their own lives. Nevertheless, there is a discomfort in the sentences. I have learned to recognize how ambivalence sounds. The tact. The not quite saying. The clotted, tangled sentences. I tell them to either give themselves permission to do it or not to do it.

You can concoct all sorts of hedges. You can tell yourself that the person you are writing about is free to write their own version, but this is a dodge because maybe they are not a writer or maybe their writing their version does not change the wrongness of yours being out in the world.

An English novelist I went out with once wrote a scene from my childhood into his novel. He gave the memory I described to him to one of his characters. I didn't much mind. I did have a twinge of thinking, *Wait, that's* mine.

In *A Charmed Life*, Mary McCarthy turned one of her friends into Dolly Lamb, whose body was "curiously flattened out, like a cloth doll that had been dressed and redressed by many imperious mistresses." That friend said later, "With her unerring accuracy, she had hit everything that was vulnerable in me, the indecisiveness of my life, the tightness of my work, my prudish habits." She also talked about feeling as though she had been "swallowed and reconstituted" by her friend. This makes innate sense to me. There is something cannibalistic about this impulse.

When writers go too far, I feel comforted by observing, *That person went too far.* I also think, *I would never go that far.* Robert Lowell, for instance, went too far when he used and re-worked his ex-wife Elizabeth Hardwick's agonized letters into the poems in *Dolphin*. His friend Elizabeth Bishop wrote to him, "One can use one's life as material—one does, anyway—but these letters—aren't you violating a trust? IF you were given permission—IF you hadn't changed them . . . etc. But *art just isn't worth that much*. . . . It makes me feel perfectly awful—to tell the truth, I feel sick for *you*."

And, as Stella might point out, what if it's not even art? What if it's just some random thing you felt like writing in a book?

In the ancient event, she was so clearly right, I was so clearly wrong. At the bookstore, she is still right, I am still wrong. It's better not to try to defend myself because there is no defense. The defenses sound false or hollow. In the end you write about something because you want to, not for any other better-sounding reason.

I stay up at night going over this incident in my head. It makes me deeply uneasy.

And yet the cannibal says, pass the arm, pass the leg.

H.'s Date

Six months after H. and I separated, I was sitting with D. at the bar of a restaurant, sharing a plate of cavatelli with sausage and drinking red wine. This was during a brief period when D. and I had broken up and were conducting some sort of tortured friendship, which included depressing dinners. Suddenly H. walked in with a tall woman in a red dress. At first it seemed impossible that this could be happening, like the universe had made a mistake that would very soon be corrected, but they sat down at a table near us and began ordering. The restaurant was about to close. After they ate, H. went out to get cash after discovering the restaurant was cash only and got locked out. The waiters were clearing and sweeping, and none of them saw him when he tried to get in. He banged on the window. He looked at us. But I told D. not to let him in. Here is a moment of pure exhilaration; I can stop time, stop him from carrying on this date, stop the inevitable end of the evening. Late that night, I realized I hadn't gotten a good look at H.'s date. Who forgets to look at her husband's date?

I think it was laziness, my tendency to picture H. as something like a weather condition, a hurricane, impossible to resist or prepare for, the path not mattering much, little aluminum-sided houses to be flooded, palm trees to tip over. This relieved me of responsibility or of, at the very least, the shame or confusion of being so passive. It's much more comforting and satisfying, of course, to think that he couldn't live with anyone, rather than the much more likely scenario that he just couldn't live with me.

I would sometimes go back over the car scene in my head. Was there another possible woman who would turn to him and say "You're kidding me" when he said "Get out," someone warm and calm and forthright, who could have joked him out of it or defused the situation? Someone steadier or sturdier? I was perversely interested in this possible rival (though of course it had been too upsetting to look directly at the real one in the restaurant.)

In the end, I hadn't asked him to leave. I'd asked him if he "wanted *to try* to work on the marriage." I did not ask him, do you want to be in the marriage. I didn't even ask him, do you want to work on the marriage. I asked him if he wanted to *try* to work on the marriage, and because he couldn't answer yes to even so-hedged and tepid a question, we both saw that he had to leave.

In the months after he moved out, I was still working on the marriage book:

> Many of the couples in the pages of this book did not recognize the shifts, and slowly accumulating distances, until it was too late. One gets from these stories a definite sense that important things happen while one is in bed with a stomach virus, or while one is straightening up and placing a pile of letters into a drawer. . . .
>
> As a union falters or fails, these writers and artists create vivid alternatives for themselves: they imagine another form of family, including friends and lovers and siblings and ex-flames, and

take from the outside world what emotional sustenance they need. Where the usual, nuclear family will not hold, they invent a structure—singular, new, innovative, often mad—that sometimes, in rare and magnificent moments, works.

I was also working on the questions: Why hadn't I extricated myself sooner? Why had I not reacted for so long? Why couldn't I give up the idea of the marriage and at least entertained the possibility of being on my own sooner? The version of myself who was worrying about the correct way to press the elevator button was not actually me, so why had I allowed her to exist and walk around and go to playgrounds and sit in libraries and shop for dinner for so long?

The Fall

One morning I am walking Violet to school. She is pushing the stroller, but I am carrying the baby because he is fussing. I am wearing pink suede three-and-a-half-inch platforms. I have a work meeting afterward, to which I am bringing the baby. My heel gets caught in the sidewalk, and I lose my balance and fall forward, somehow managing to put both my arms up and cup my hands around the baby's head so my legs and arms are badly scraped and bruised but the baby is untouched. He is crying but only out of outrage at such a sudden and undignified change of position.

Of course a crowd gathers. A woman carrying a newborn has fallen and is bleeding. Violet is beyond mortified, and people are in no way leaving us alone. She is actually trying to stand a little away from us so that she won't be associated with us, but being six, with only limited success. I try to respond politely to the concern while also trying to get away from the people so Violet can stop dying of embarrassment.

She is right to be angry. I wore the heels the same way I wore stilettos to parties nine months pregnant, in defiance of the laws of nature, and this time it endangered the baby, who she only sort of thinks of as mine and mostly thinks of as hers.

Later I will tell this as a funny story, which is a way of hiding, or a magical-instincts-of-motherhood story, which is another way of hiding. I never tell it as a story about how reckless or selfish I am and how these various roles I am trying to play are fundamentally not conducive to staying upright on earth.

I see myself suddenly from the perspective of one of the women rushing to work who stopped on the street: vain, anxious, overcaffeinated, narcissistic, unable to give up men looking at her on the street for even the first few months of her baby's life. Trying too hard. Trying too flagrantly. Clinging too tenaciously to the most hackneyed and unsubtle indicator of female sexual power.

I think, not for the first time, why am I allowed to have this baby? I would not at this point be entirely surprised if someone in a uniform came and took him away.

A couple of months earlier, one of my male colleagues swung by my office. Noticing that I was visibly pregnant with no man in my life, he said, "Wow, you really do whatever you want." I laughed, of course, but the comment stayed with me, the admiration but also the warning undertones, that I was getting away with something that you usually can't get away with, being a sexual free agent *and* having a baby. As if I were shoplifting the baby, getting him for free.

Violet goes right to the heart of it: "Why are you wearing those shoes?" At six, she wears exclusively sports clothes, soccer jerseys, and sneakers. She has not missed the sea of Brooklyn mothers in sneakers, in silver Birkenstocks, in ballet flats—which in particular seem to telegraph some sort of shimmering apex of female serenity I will never attain—and are not, at 8:20 a.m., trying to impress anyone.

Germaine Greer: "Women with more pride than libido do not see their emancipation from the duty of sexual attraction as death-in-life."

Doris Lessing: "You only begin to discover the difference between what you really are, your real self, and your appearance when you get a bit older . . . a whole dimension of life suddenly slides away and you realize that what in fact you've been using to get attention has been what you look like . . . it really is a most salutary and fascinating thing to go through, shedding it all."

The true power must be in not caring how you look when you have slept maybe three hours. But I am seduced by surfaces, by habit, by the mysteriously lingering imperative to be recognizably me. The baby is fine, thank god, but he won't always be or could so easily not have been. The bruises declare themselves in festive yellows, greens, mauves.

reads out loud from a book the size of her palm, *You can only live your own life. Stop trying to live other people's lives.* The feeling of running someone else's life or fixing or helping or managing is itself addictive, a drug that holds all kinds of screeching demons at bay, the same way that Vicodin or vodka does for the addict. *Don't pick up,* they say in the rooms.

The Thursday Meeting

I try substituting "random amoral fate" for "higher power." It still pretty much works. I can turn the problem over to random amoral fate. One of my new Al-Anon friends has another way of putting this: "not my department."

We are sitting in a large circle on folding chairs in a pretty church you enter through a garden of candy-colored tulips. Someone reads from a laminated sheet, *We admitted we are powerless over alcohol.* Or Vicodin or heroin or whatever it is. *That our lives had become unmanageab* Though this doesn't sound on the surface like good news, it's calm Here is something you can't control: someone else's self-destr behavior.

The room is hot. I am still not a hundred percent convinc is not a cult. But I feel so much better sitting here that I to walk out.

People toss around words and phrases I don't kno in a foreign country and can't read the street si something deeply familiar: I had an addict in and have a recovering addict in my house n

One of the central ideas of the progran things you can't control. To be releas

The Call

I am making coffee, getting ready to go to work, when the landline, which no one ever uses, rings.

"Hello, Katie?" says a strange English accent.

"Yes . . . who is this?"

"I'd rather not say. I am just calling to apologize because I was sleeping with [the Claw] while you were with him."

Pause.

"That was two years ago."

"Yes, but I feel bad now. I realize now that I was doing something awful to you and I owe you an apology."

"But you don't even know me."

"Well, I feel like I do. I know so much about you."

"Are you in London?"

"No, but it's *so interesting* that you would think that. I just am very, very sorry. I wanted to reach out and apologize to you."

"Well, we didn't have a monogamous arrangement, so I really don't think you have anything to apologize—"

"That's so nice of you to say. It's so good to finally hear your voice. I have heard so much about you, from him, of course, and from other people. He showed me your emails. I'm friends with some of your students. I am just surprised that you are being so nice. I didn't realize you were going to be so nice."

"Well, there are a lot of reasons that relationship didn't work out, so there's really no reason for you to feel bad about it. We were together for almost two years, and I never even introduced him to my children."

Why was I telling her this? Why was I trying to make this anonymous caller feel better? Why was I still on the phone?

"I know what it feels like now, because now I am in your position. For a while, I had, you know, the glow of his attention, and now I don't, so I suddenly understand how you must have felt."

I hadn't thought about the Claw for a while. Susan Sontag once wrote, "I change countries as easily as I change rooms," and the Claw was like that. He flew so constantly that his life was flight; he conducted his human relationships in the ambiance of an airport lounge; he set up different little provisional worlds in different cities and left as soon as any one of them got too serious or stable or intense. He was both gifted at and panicked by intimacy. He was responsible to no one, beholden to no one, faithless, family-less, in a hotel room or borrowed flat, drinking good red wine, alone. (Or was he not alone? I guess that was the problem.)

Tall with lots of gray-black hair, he dressed formally but sometimes wore cowboy boots. He was twenty years older than me. A dinner party at his house is the only time I can remember feeling intimidated by a conversation: the casual references to philosophers, quotes from Jorge Luis Borges or Elias Canetti, lapses into at least three other languages, savage charismatic mockery of mutual acquaintances. I felt like a twelve-year-old at a dinner of slightly terrifying adults. The

Claw had inherited enough money and art from his intellectual parents not to have to worry about boring things like working.

Our first kiss seemed like it might be based on a misunderstanding. In the taxi home at midnight, I had to go over the kiss in my head, "What did that mean?" as if there were other meanings I couldn't quite think of and might possibly uncover.

The Claw and I never went out. We sat in his baroquely cluttered loft, lined with library bookcases with ladders up to the ceiling. He said he had guns stashed away somewhere, but I never saw one. We drank bottles of champagne and ate bar snacks, pretzels, nuts, little sesame things, and rice crackers. We almost never committed to anything as serious as dinner. I never introduced him to any of my friends. I never introduced him to my children. He stepped foot in my house only once in the nearly two years we were together. It was like having an affair with a married person, only neither of us was married. It was like having an affair with a married person on an island.

He liked to say that he didn't believe in "conjugal life," the phrase itself implying that the whole idea of marrying or living with someone was hopelessly antiquated and outmoded and clunky, rather than, say, something nearly everybody at some point or another did. To his credit, the Claw presented all kinds of warning labels and disclaimers up front: He was not interested in monogamy. He was not interested in having any children in his life. He believed all marriages and long-term relationships were unhappy or ordinary or drab or restless, though he was shrewd enough to present himself as damaged, to say that settled life was "beyond him," as if he were a monster roaming the earth alone, silhouetted against ice caps. The first night we were together, I broke a champagne glass in his house by accident.

One day, he emailed me some lines of a James Fenton poem that had "popped into" his head: "Beauty, danger and dismay/Met me on the public way./Whichever I chose, I chose dismay."

I didn't mind all this. I may have even liked it. In the five years since I had separated from my husband, I had lost track of what it meant to live with another adult, to compromise, to bend, to change, to apologize, to bicker, to have someone bring you tea when you are sick, to go to bed angry.

I understood the exhilaration of compartments, of having everything in its place. I was used to, even quasireligious about, keeping my stable, domestic sphere with my children entirely separate from the men I was involved with, fleetingly or otherwise.

It seems to me even now that this is not necessarily a bad way to live with very small children, to spend most of the week cleaning broccoli florets crushed onto a high chair and then to get dressed up and escape to a man's house, have a glass of wine, or many glasses, and then return in the same clothes, happily exhausted, the next morning. It still strikes me as in many ways civilized to separate love and baby care, in ways some young parents under the same roof occasionally try to do but can't, finding themselves miraculously transported to a dark restaurant, candles flickering, with blood orange martinis or caipirinhas, mulling over the merits of a particular babysitter.

A friend of mine nicknamed him "the Claw" early on, to defend against my already alarming infatuation and evoke his unnatural hold on me. We always referred to him as the Claw, e.g., "I am going to have a drink with the Claw" or "Did you see the Claw this weekend?" as a way of taming him, of, I guess, declawing him. The name implied a deformity, a monstrousness that seemed fair, simultaneously romanticizing him and cutting him down.

Did I care that he might be with other women? The situation was particularly maddening for me because I wanted to be the person who doesn't care, who is so consummately secure that she is not threatened, whose life is so full and engaging that she does not think about where a man is when he is not with her, but the truth is that I was not precisely or was not always that person.

In the marriage book, I had written about the couples: "They believed in improvising the old form, in creating relationships like art, in experimenting in love in all sorts of colorful and dubious ways, and yet they could not entirely elude the primal allure of the past. At least three of the women who appear in these pages lived with a rather large amount of sexual disorder, and maintained a secret passion for Jane Austen."

It seems possible that I didn't wholly want anything more consuming or traditional because I didn't have energy or time or space for that, especially with the baby. It's also possible that I liked the feeling of briefly possessing someone so promiscuous, and any evidence of his wildness made my brief possession more exciting or interesting. Still, I wanted more of him than he wanted of me.

Of course, radical freedom works better for a man on his own than a woman with two children, one of them under two. I couldn't convincingly be even a little free. I couldn't meet someone for coffee without planning it with military precision. I had a few flings of my own, perfunctory ones, but there were meters running, babysitters waiting, during the time that I could tolerate being away from the baby, which was not, to be honest, a very long time.

The Claw's glamorous nihilism about all human attachments attracted me: how few illusions he entertained about relationships, how little of the impingements of other people he could tolerate, how many dinners he skipped out on at the last minute, how many friends and colleagues and work parties he ducked, how radically unencumbered he was, how little he compromised on his work or did things he didn't want to do, because he had money of his own.

It wasn't only that I wanted him, of course; it was that I wanted to *be* him. What would it be like not to be obligated to other people or to skip out on that obligation whenever you felt like it? Being with the Claw was like taking an intense, intellectually flashy crash course in how not to care what other people think.

But did I mind his sleeping with other women? It's strange that I can't answer such a basic question more easily. I liked the idea of myself not minding. Not that I was pretending or papering over or acting a part. I couldn't separate my own desires from his, or rather I couldn't tolerate the idea of losing him, so I became someone he could keep around. I liked the partial and intermittent him better than the whole and constant someone else.

One day, the Claw tells me that I've left a pair of underwear in his bed. When he hands me the freshly laundered size XS dove gray lace panties, they are not mine. I don't say anything. The awfulness of the moment belongs to me and not him. That's how it feels, as if it is somehow my fault that they are not mine. As if I am needlessly stirring up trouble. I take them home but am unsure what to do with them. I put them in the back of a closet.

Simone de Beauvoir #1

Open relationships have always confused me, specifically Simone de Beauvoir's relationship with Jean-Paul Sartre, in which they both had other very compelling loves, sometimes the same woman. He argued that jealousy was narrow and bourgeois, a position that she, with some effort, took up. "At times," she wrote, "I asked myself whether the whole of my happiness did not rest upon a gigantic lie."

I have heard people smooth over the complexities and argue that she was living a life she knowingly and fully chose. They also argue that she enjoyed and reveled in and fully availed herself of the openness of their situation. All true. But if someone had offered her the possibility of having Sartre all to herself all the time, there is at least very strong evidence that she would have taken it.

She was a connoisseur of female abjection, a brilliant elucidator of it. Her novels and stories are filled with elaborately pining women, the unloved, the cheated on, the shunted to the side, who are not her; but she was elaborately convincing on the topic of loving a man who didn't love you back with the same devotion or constancy. A character in one of her novels observes, "It's restful to have someone entirely to yourself."

There are moments, mostly wordless, where she seems to suffer. There are days that she walks around crying, to parties, to Café de Flore, to dinners with friends, "she would almost suffocate with sobbing," someone observes; there are the crippling headaches she got, provoked by Sartre's persistent devotion to his actress girlfriend, Wanda, but then she makes or wills herself into another, slightly different version of herself who is fine.

After hearing about Sartre's passion for his early paramour, Olga, she writes "The agony which this produced in me went far beyond mere jealousy." But there is also, as she probably felt, a perverse kind of pleasure to this kind of suffering, to picturing someone you want to be with in someone else's arms. Jealousy can be energizing, picturing something painful to you and then forcing yourself to unpicture it; to get past it, to wade or reason your way through it, can feel like an accomplishment. After all the ordeals, she writes to him, their love is like a hard diamond.

She is beautiful, queenly, commanding, dark hair piled on top of her head, arched eyebrows, red lipstick, white blouses, fur coats. He is beastish, about five feet tall, teddy bear shaped, glasses, bad teeth, bad skin. One day they have this exchange, which Beauvoir records for posterity:

HER: Were you ever attracted by an ugly woman?

HIM: Truly and wholly ugly, no, never.

HER: It could even be said that all the women you were fond of were either distinctly pretty, or at least very attractive and full of charm.

HIM: Yes, in our relations, I liked a woman to be pretty because it was a way of developing my sensibility.

HER: Were there not women you found attractive for reasons other than strictly feminine qualities—strength of character, something intellectual and mental, rather than something wholly to do with charm and femininity?

Wishful thinking. Her contempt for some of his flimsier love interests comes through in *The Second Sex*, where she writes of men generally, "He dreams of what she might have been, of what she perhaps will be: she can be credited with any possibilities, because she *is* nothing in particular. This vacancy is what makes the lover weary of her quickly; but it is the source of the mystery, the charm, that seduces him and makes him inclined to feel an easy affection in the first place."

She provoked and disturbed feminists with her famous comment about her relationship with Sartre: "There has been one undoubted success in my life: my relationship with Sartre." I can almost understand. She adapts her whole being to the situation. She will not be hurt because she will change herself like a sculptor working in clay. She labors for it, sacrifices for it. It is an achievement, a consummately creative act: she invents herself in it.

Like the French feminists, I would, of course, rather think of her working at a cluttered desk, her scribbled notes stained with rings from coffee cups, not thinking about him. I would prefer to think of her not caring whether he went away with a particular woman for three weeks or five weeks, rather than pleading and bargaining and negotiating for extra days; I prefer to think of her not canceling months of a trip she had planned with another man to wander through Mexico because Sartre suddenly told her he wanted her around. She drops everything for him, every time. On the other hand, this is what she wanted, the sometimes pain of a strong emotion over the muffled comfort of an easier one.

But still, the sensible feminists would say, is that relationship a more superb achievement, a greater success, than her novel *The Mandarins*, than the dazzling world-roiling international classic *The Second Sex*? Maybe it is. She writes, "For me a choice is never made, it is always being made . . . the horror of the definitive choice is that it engages not only the self of today, but that of tomorrow, which is why basically marriage is immoral."

In a particularly loveless moment, she wrote to an ex-flame, "A woman cannot live without some passion. As love is forbidden, I decided to give my dirty heart to something not so piggish as a man: and I gave myself a nice beautiful black car."

There is a photo of Simone de Beauvoir in her forties naked in a bathroom that I love. We see her from the back, at the sink, pinning up her hair, wearing nothing but heels. At the time, she was taken by surprise by the photographer, who had not asked permission, but in the photo itself she doesn't care about him or anything. She is just putting herself together.

Insomnia

Everyone in my household has insomnia. At one in the morning, the baby, one and a half now, calls out from his crib, "Where is my mama? Where is my mango? Where is my ketchup?"

Where I am is in bed, worrying about money, scrolling through bills in my head, while my real bills are piling up unopened, as if they only become problems if I open the envelopes. I repress, among other things, the US mail.

Before I started teaching, I told myself that I needed a job or a husband, and a job seemed less onerous. It took a long time to find one. Now I am up for tenure at the university. If you get tenure you have a job forever, and if you don't get tenure you lose your job immediately.

I have a recurring dream that we live in a giant furnished cardboard box, serrated windows cut unevenly in a sloppy child's imitation of a real house. This is not a subtle dream. I recognize the melodrama even as I am dreaming, *Oh, come on*. And yet, even after I wake up, the terror lingers.

One frigid January day, the boiler breaks, and while I am calling someone to come fix it, a pipe explodes. The sound is like a gunshot. A sheet of water, a waterfall, cascades down the yellow wall of Violet's room. For a minute, I think, *Yes, now it is happening*. My neighbors, two handsome brothers who are contractors, come and turn off the water in the basement. We all mop. Soaked towels are crumpled on the floor. The Sheetrock is damp and possibly molding and, one of the contractors points out, likely to damage the brains of the children. But I feel the panic subside. It's over. The house will not be falling apart today.

One day I write a newspaper article, "In Defense of Single Mothers." The editor sends me the final proofs. While I look over my words, set in the familiar newspaper type, I have a moment of thinking, if I put this in print I will always be single. The words in newsprint make it true, claim me.

I go to dinner with a man, and afterward we sit on the couch in his dark, empty living room and watch an episode of *Orange Is the New Black*. It seems so exotic and strange, this feeling of sitting next to someone watching something, that I think, "Who does this?" and then remember, "Oh, everyone."

After his wife died, Julian Barnes wrote, "I have lots of people to do something with but I have no one to do nothing with."

I am totally transfixed by articles about tiny apartments or micro-houses, especially by photographs of the immaculate space, two hundred and fifty square feet, a bed folding out from the wall, an espresso maker, modern stools tucked under a narrow wooden table, a giant square window onto implausibly verdant green woods. I feel an odd, powerful sense of recognition, as if I have spent years in this micro-house, as if important events unspooled in it. As if my own bed folded into the wall. I think this is because this phase is requiring cutting out excess, winnowing down, paring down to essentials. In fact, it's myself I have folded and collapsed and made efficient.

I am friends with single mothers who have quietly stopped viewing their single-mother phase as temporary or accidental, who have, without balloons or trumpets, definitively shifted into a permanent-seeming state. One of them is chided by her therapist: "You aren't going to meet someone between the kitchen and the living room."

As single mothers, we are autocrats in our tiny republics. Men, in this context, become extra, unnecessary, an interesting luxury. The idea of accommodating one seems eccentric or pioneering or, in any event, extreme.

I like the improvised picnic feel of being one adult alone with children. I crave and am maybe addicted to this feeling; a man in my house would shift the focus, would normalize the household, would diminish it.

James Baldwin: "The roles that we construct are constructed because we feel that they will help us to survive and also, of course, because they fulfill something in our personalities; and one does not, therefore, cease playing a role because one has begun to understand it. All roles are dangerous. The world tends to trap and immobilize you in the role you play; and it is not always easy— in fact, it is always extremely hard—to maintain a kind of watchful, mocking distance between oneself as one appears to be and oneself as one actually is."

My friends seem to think of me as extremely competent, which confuses me because everything feels makeshift, improvised, fly by night.

On Sunday nights, everything falls extravagantly apart over the stupidest, most trivial thing. We take the subway to the Upper West Side, have dinner at my mother's house, and then it gets late and I pile everyone into a taxi, and the children fall asleep draped all over me, and when we get home, I wake them up, and they cry hysterically, and I try to hold the baby with one arm while getting the stroller and various bags out of the trunk with the other, Violet sobbing and sort of crumpling, barely able to stand on the curb, and me shepherding everyone to the door, and fumbling to find my key in the darkness, both children wailing, and me not being able to see the lock because the outside bulb has burned out, but not having a hand to hold my phone up for light so I can't for the life of me get the key into the lock.

Standing in the dark at the iron-gated door, I get a wave of nostalgia for a state I was never frankly in, a big benign husband carrying sleeping children in and unlocking the door and turning on lights. The outside bulb has burned out and has been waiting for me to find the wherewithal to change it for what is approaching two years now. Some things, I have accepted, are beyond me, and this particular lightbulb, now coated in a layer of dirt and cobwebs and interesting insects, is for its own reasons beyond me, and probably always will be. The gate is stuck and slightly rusted, and in the time it takes to get the lock open I am wondering: What deep security am I withholding from the children?

When I finally get in, everyone still howling, I put the kids into bed, in their clothes, without brushing their teeth, and the cavities they are probably getting seem sinister; I can't believe my hubris—an exflame used the word "hubris" to describe my thinking I could successfully manage a baby alone—and delusion in thinking I could do this on my own when I so obviously can't, and everything comes crashing down. And this loneliness, which distills, finally, into the basic practical need for another pair of arms, if I were a Hindu god with four blue curling bangled arms, that would solve the problem too, undoes me.

In the light of day, it's hard to understand why I am derailed by a tiny thing like getting out of a taxi on a Sunday night. Of course, right behind the fear that I can't manage on my own is another more terrifying fear: that I can.

I am not looking. I am not happy or unhappy. It is like a peace treaty has been signed without my realizing it. The restlessness a former version of myself would have felt has been pushed away, repurposed into efficiency.

It is an intoxicating feeling, not needing anyone, but also isolating in itself. I imagine this is how runners feel on a windy day on the beach, though I have never been a runner: hard, strong, lean, sinewy. The mood is of traveling light.

I have become someone who lives alone. I remember sitting cross-legged for games of "old maid" as a child, the horror of being stuck with the prim witchy woman card, the hot shame of it.

Olivia Laing: "I was keeling toward the midpoint of my thirties, an age at which female aloneness is no longer socially sanctioned and carries with it a persistent whiff of strangeness, deviance and failure."

But I like hanging around in the kitchen with the kids, having a glass of wine standing up while they eat buttery pasta.

"You need to go out," my mother tells me on the phone. "But why?" I would ask her, if it wouldn't upset her too much. I can't remember why I need to go out.

My Mother #1

Maybe my mother's voice is in my head because I talk to her nearly every day. If any of us makes the mistake of saying we like something of hers, she will try to give it to us. One cold day after H. moved out, when I hadn't pulled myself together to get Violet warm clothes, she heard a note of panic in my voice and got onto the subway with three beautiful toddler-sized sweaters. She will drop anything for me or my sisters, support us in anything, defend us against anyone.

But without ever saying it out loud, she makes known very early on that she will not consider my life successful or full unless or until I have a man in it. By this she does not mean men, the ad hoc situations I fall into every now and then. She means a permanent, more traditional, preferably lawful partner. She can't think of me as happy or secure without one.

This could be surprising because my mother was an ardent feminist when I was growing up, carting three-year-old me in striped Oshkosh overalls to marches for women's rights, hand-lettered signs aloft in the crowd: A WOMAN NEEDS A MAN LIKE A FISH NEEDS A BICYCLE. I remember loving that slogan, the cartoon charisma of it, the picture of the fish atop a bicycle. Back then, my mother had a giant mass of short curly hair, a flowing sundress, sandals.

If a man sits next to her, my mother, who has let her hair go white, will become luminous. She grew up with the skill of drawing a man out, making him comfortable, mixing him a sidecar or Manhattan or martini, something she learned to do at age eight. Her mother trained her. She can make any man of any age as comfortable as he has ever been anywhere. Even in her eighties, she can make him feel admired, seen, cherished, in under ten minutes. I have watched her do it. It's impressive to behold.

Virginia Woolf: "Women have served all these centuries as looking-glasses possessing the magic and delicious power of reflecting the figure of a man as twice its natural size. Without that power probably the earth would still be swamp and jungle."

Once after a surgery my mother had in her late seventies, a mysterious man none of us had ever heard of showed up with a giant box with a red ribbon around it, containing a plush bathrobe from Bergdorf's; even in a hospital bed, tubes coming out of her arms, she had suitors showing up, even in extremis some man is always in the process of being charmed.

For my mother, the old order lingers. She would never think of going to a restaurant alone and sitting at the bar and ordering a hamburger. She would never think of asking for more money for something she wrote (she recently surprised me with her medieval vehemence on this point: "I would rather cut out my own tongue"). She is not beyond pretending she doesn't understand something so that a man can explain it to her, "mansplaining" to her being a useful device a woman can manipulate toward her own ends. For a while this felt to me like an unfair bait and switch. But at some point I figured out that there is no point in trying to wrench consistency or logic from her. She was raised in the forties and fifties. I am not sure that even an intense political awakening can entirely undo decades of cultural messaging, her father saying to her, "Only ugly women become lawyers." Somewhere there underneath everything, single women are trolls, freaks.

I have a sense that while I am single, anything I can achieve only partially counts. She will still be thinking somewhere under everything that I am unhappy. I have the feeling that I can write books or magazine articles or get tenure, but none of it will please her (and by please, of course, I mean release her from her endless cycle of worrying about me) the way a husband or at least a man in my house would. There is something incomplete about me, about my family, unfinished. She loyally supported my choice to have a baby on my own, but she would not think that it was fine to go on that way.

She herself lived alone in the sixties after her alcoholic, flagrantly philandering first husband ran off. She must have felt this same intoxicating relief, the open road even single mothers of small children feel when they are not too exhausted. She owned a rabbit named Alouette who ate the bindings of her books and chewed through her rattan furniture. She cut her hair Mia Farrow short and wore a short dress with a daisy print on it and pretended to inhale cigarettes and pushed my sister in her stroller and left her to nap on piles of coats at parties. She slept with interesting men. But for her this is the in-between phase. She met my father, a doctor, and settled into a house, and had more children and dogs, and in her narrative that's when her real life began.

When one of my good friends gets divorced, my mother says, "Oh, I am sure she will meet someone right away." There is layered into this comment a barbed comparison to me, who years later—even, one might point out, *a baby later*—has not "met someone," or rather who has met many someones who are just passing through.

Why can't I block her out? These occasional wounding or belittling comments. Somehow a mother's view has an irrational ascendance, you can rationalize it away all you want, but it rises up like a neon billboard in the night sky.

Nearly a decade later, Violet will be sitting on a white furry beanbag chair, working on a history research paper on sixteenth-century witch hunts in Europe. She will have laid out all her notecards about how the women most vulnerable to the accusations were unattached, widows, spinsters. They were thought to have sex with the Devil at night. I will have a chill of recognition. In my head, I know those clucking towns-people, secretly suspicious of those single women, thinking to them-selves, "I always thought there was something not quite right about her."

Sometimes, sitting on the floor, following very confusing instructions, and creating a very complicated Lego *Star Wars* ship with Leo, which is not my forte, or having an Ikea desk, late at night, miraculously permit itself to be assembled, I feel a flash of pride and surprise at my competence. *See, I don't need a man!* But then quickly I hear my mother's voice. Disaster looms. Something I can't manage is about to happen. Something I can't fix is breaking. I am not permitted by the universe that feeling of self-sufficiency, that comfort. The fish, it turns out, needs a bicycle.

The Wednesday Meeting

Someone is talking about her sister's overdose. "I had seen her a few days before. I thought she was doing a little better."

I think of seeing my sister on heroin. Seeing her disappear in front of me. Her eyelids fluttering so I can see the whites. It feels otherworldly, religious almost. I am twelve.

One thing that is scary is that I don't know what to do with this information. I do not think I should tell my parents because they will be upset.

All these years later, I mention this memory to my mother over lunch. She says, "That never happened." But when we go over the chronology, she concedes that it might have: my sister was doing heroin and living under our roof in precisely those years. Then she changes the subject.

This feeling that something out of control is happening but not acknowledged. There is some shouting about my sister, but it is not about this. This thing is not put into words in a house in which everything under the sun is put into words. I do not know if my parents know or don't know, but this is not something that we talk about out loud. Everything is all right in our house, with two dogs, two cats, two turtles, two guinea pigs, five sisters, but this one thing which is not all right. I, meanwhile, am writing a play about the Scarsdale diet doctor who was murdered by his girlfriend, Jean Harris, who was deranged with anger about his affairs and possibly suicidal. When my friends and I put on a performance, I play Jean Harris.

Other things come back to me in the rooms. The day my sister convinced me that she was part mermaid because she could stay under water for so long. The day she came home after putting her arms down on the grill of one of the halal pushcarts in Washington Square Park. The day she stole a painting off the wall of our house, of a sallow woman in a red beret, and sold it to a gallery. The time she was staying in an East Village apartment without a door. She brought with her so much crisis that the rest of us had to always be fine to make up for my mother's unhappinesses. These rooms are for the one who is always "fine."

Last year my sister had a brain hemorrhage so massive it would have killed most people. They airlifted her from her remote town in New Mexico to a hospital in Albuquerque, where she was in a coma. When I flew to see her, she had just regained consciousness. In the neurological intensive care unit, coming out of it, a shunt in her partially shaved head, she was delivering funny and erudite disquisitions on Japanese film and Philip Roth and Anne Frank and which of the variety of cacti in New Mexico were somehow obscene, to the bewildered nurses. She is always the most charismatic person in a room.

Someone is talking about perfectionism: "I felt like if I got all As in school, if I excelled at everything and won prizes, my father would stop doing drugs. Our house would stop being the meth house." If something out of control is scaring you, you can be perfect. "Of course," the woman goes on, "I was never perfect. There is always more I could do. And even if I was somehow able to be perfect, my father would not stop doing drugs. Even if I was perfect, he would not love me. It took me a long time to figure that one out. To stop trying."

Relatable

My students love to talk about a writer being "relatable." Can't something be good or fascinating without your identifying with the writer? I ask them. They can appreciate a piece of writing if it's not "relatable," I notice, but they can't love it. They know all of my objections to the word, but they can't stop themselves from using it in class. Zadie Smith is relatable. Leslie Jamison is relatable. Roxane Gay is relatable. Even Joan Didion, having dinner with movie stars in expensive restaurants in Los Angeles, is relatable to students living with four roommates in Bushwick above a doughnut shop.

The pressure for women to "be honest," by which people nearly always mean be vulnerable, show weakness, soften the edges, sound like you are not totally pulled together, confess that you are drinking too much, say, or crying in the street, or stylishly neurotic à la Joan Didion or suffering with an eating disorder or struggling with depression is a very powerful one. But something in me resists.

I can see that the "I" in most of my pieces is not relatable. If anything, she is ferocious. If my not-relating students asked, I would try to explain that she is not precisely or wholly me, that she seems instead the best way of putting out my ideas: a vehicle, a tank.

Many people will find this kind of writing off-putting. Strong interpretations or opinions or worldviews are somehow better received if they are couched in approachability. The writer has to telegraph "I am a mess" to mitigate an otherwise arrogant or chafing presumption. Especially if the writer is a woman.

Virginia Woolf: "It was impossible to make head or tail of it all, I decided, glancing with envy at the reader next door who was making the neatest abstracts, headed often with an A or a B or a C, while my own notebook rioted with the wildest scribble of contradictory jottings. It was distressing, it was bewildering, it was humiliating. Truth had run through my fingers. Every drop had escaped. . . . It was disgraceful to have nothing more weighty or respectable to show after a whole morning's work." Or: "Alas, laid on the grass how small, how insignificant this thought of mine looked; the sort of fish that a good fisherman puts back into the water so that it may grow fatter and be one day worth cooking and eating. I will not trouble you with that thought now."

Mary McCarthy: "Whenever I became tight I would bring up (oh, *vino veritas*) the Tsar and his family. I did not see why they all had to be killed. . . . The next morning I was always bitterly ashamed. I had let these omniscient men see the real me underneath, and the other me squirmed and gritted her teeth and muttered, Never, never, *never* again."

It is a ritual, this performance of weakness, these protestations of being just like everyone else (say, drunk at a party, hung over and regretful afterward). Authority can be seized, it sometimes feels, only if it is playfully, skillfully warded away at the same time.

I start to think of these moments, these deferrals of power as "I-am-a-mess" moments. (Everyone is, after all, a mess. The question is whether you want to announce or billboard it in your writing.)

Zadie Smith: "One September night, running home from dinner to meet a babysitter, I took off my heels and hopped barefoot—it was raining—up Crosby Street, and so home. *Hepatitis*, I thought. Hep-a-ti-tis. I reached my building bedraggled, looking like death. The doorman—who'd complimented me on my way out—blushed and looked down at his smart phone." A little later on, she tells us that she drank too much vodka and would rather be on her iPhone than read. She begins another essay, "It might be useful to distinguish between pleasure and joy. But maybe everybody does this very easily, all the time, and only I am confused."

Leslie Jamison: "Getting blackout drunk and sharing my feelings in fleeting pockets of lucidity; sleeping with guys and crying in their bathrooms afterward." And: "Down in the basement, before I tossed it, I scooped out some peanut butter with my fingers and ate it in gobs. Then I threw the jar away. Then I went back to the elevator. Then I returned to the dumpster, found the jar, twisted it open, and stuck my fingers in it again. That was the truth of me: not this skinny girl who never ate but that girl with dirty fingers, leaning into the trash."

Roxane Gay: "Ten minutes before my first class I run into the bathroom and vomit. I'm afraid of public speaking, which makes teaching complicated. When I walk into the classroom the students stare at me like I am in charge. They stare at me and wait for me to say something. I stare back and wait for them to do something. . . . I have no idea how I got to be the one in front of the classroom, the one who gets to be in charge of things."

Joan Didion: "I cried until I was not even aware when I was crying and when I was not, cried in elevators and in taxis and in Chinese laundries, and when I went to the doctor he said only that I seemed to be depressed. . . . Of course I could not work. I could not even get dinner with any degree of certainty, and I would sit in the apartment on Seventy-fifth Street paralyzed until my husband would call from his office and say gently that I did not have to get dinner, that I could meet him at Michael's Pub or at Toots Shor's or at Sardi's East."

I am not suggesting that any of these writers has adopted a conscious strategy. The instinct is so deep and ingrained that it is inseparable from personality or style itself. We all do some version of this in the course of an average day: diffuse competition, brush off compliments, be self-deprecating, anticipate and dismantle the question "What makes her think she is so special?" before it even begins to form in someone's head. Protestations of disorganization, of not being pulled together, these are such common currency in female interaction that we are barely even aware of them. One woman saying "You look great," the other saying, without thinking, "Oh, I haven't slept in forever. I have the hugest circles under my eyes. "

Leslie Jamison writes beautifully about her cutting, drinking till she passes out, anorexia. When one reads her description of these episodes, one feels immediately protective. Jamison has become a vulnerable person to be shielded by our goodwill. Her words operate almost to defuse a bomb. She is not just impressive with her gorgeous turns of phrase, her breadth of references. To be merely impressive would awaken a dangerous competitiveness, perhaps putting us on edge, by being so smart, by analyzing things so astutely, so sharply, as if from above. Instead she is relatable, struggling. She is *getting blackout drunk and sharing my feelings in fleeting pockets of lucidity; sleeping with guys and crying in their bathrooms afterward.* She is reaching into the garbage to eat peanut butter with her hands. She is still impressive, but she has made or rendered herself likable, less threatening. She reports one of her boyfriends saying to her that he likes her when she is drunk because then she is just as stupid as everyone else. This same reassuring, equalizing principle is at work when she writes about her drinking.

There is, of course, nothing wrong with sharing vulnerabilities as one form of intimacy among many. But not as an imperative, not as a rule, not as an almost cultural demand made on female writing.

Mary Beard on women and power: "We may sincerely want them to get to the inside of it or we may, by various often unconscious means, cast women as interlopers when they make it."

Why this punishing competiveness? Do we still feel like there is not enough for all of us (not enough attention; not enough money; not enough love; not enough spoils)? That other women, if they have power, may take what is or could be ours? Virginia Woolf wrote eloquently in *A Room of One's Own* about the feeling of not enough, of scarcity, of the dinner of prunes and dry biscuits and plain soup at the women's college compared to the abundant, heartwarming dinner at the men's college. She contrasts "the safety and prosperity of the one sex, and the poverty and insecurity of the other."

One learns from girlhood to fear the competitive energy, the ambient fury and resentment that can be aimed at powerful females. And yet at the same time, women often want or need power. The goal, then, is to take power in a way that navigates that rage or resentment; it is a little like trying to feed a dragon without getting burned.

In 1961, Elizabeth Hardwick wrote about the necessity for women writers to "soften the scandal of the action or courage of opinion." She wrote that "Madame de Staël, vexing and far-out as she was, needed her rather embarrassing love affairs to smooth over, like a cosmetic cream, the shrewd image."

I can think of a handful of women writers who resist "I-am-a-mess" moments. Susan Sontag and Janet Malcolm come immediately to mind, but there are very few (Sontag really, really did not like weakness; she went so far as to write in her notebooks, "Weakness is contagion. Strong people rightly shun the weak.") These two writers are somehow not promising friendship, offering a cup of coffee; they are not *relating*, not apologizing.

Hillary Clinton: "What could I do to be 'more real'? Dance on a table? Swear a blue streak? Break down sobbing? That's not me." She knows exactly what is wrong with the image she has put out into the world. She knows what's behind the almost existential discomfort with her. In order to atone or compensate for her power, the public wants to see her break down, lose control.

I would like to ask my students, "What if the writer doesn't feel like showing weakness? What if she is doing some other thing?" What if her interest is not in your relating to her as a friend you could confide in, but in your confrontation with her ideas?

We often describe women who write about pain or vulnerabilities as "brave," but this type of confession is so frequently exchanged, so par for the course, so deeply and comfortably ensconced in the language of female confidences, so nearly de rigueur in the kind of personal writing ascendant now, so deeply woven into the way women get along with each other in the world generally that bravery may not be quite the right word. It is, in a way, something more like capitulating.

Of course, I also want to capitulate. I give a friend an essay I've written about divorce. Is it too cold? Too sharp? Too angry? Too abrasive? She answers tactfully, "I think you might seem a little less, um, harsh if you put in something about forgetting to pack Violet's lunch or buying her a scone because you were too late to give her breakfast and getting disgusting crumbs mashed into the stroller." She is trying to say that I would come across as more likable if I presented myself as a little bit of a mess, if I showed more weakness, and I know she is probably right. She brightens. "Maybe you could put in a scene where you are crying?"

I tell my friend I will try. I start to type a crying scene, but it sounds awkward, as if I am making it up. Why can't I write it more convincingly? Because something in me stiffens, rebels. The sentence is clotted, false, because I do not want to put it on the page.

One reason I don't present myself as crying as I walk down the street or on men's bathroom floors is that I don't generally cry as I walk down the street or on men's bathroom floors. But my instinct with pain or vulnerability is to hide or bury. I don't even show it to myself.

Here is something true I could have put in the divorce piece: "It some-times feels like he has blanked out everything. He has fallen so sud-denly out of love with me, like a water faucet turned off, that it seems tantalizingly possible that he will fall back in love with me just as sud-denly. I put photographs of the two of us in a box, letters, postcards, and give it to him. I seem to think all that is required is proof. As if he has somehow forgotten." But I don't put anything like this in the article.

Simone de Beauvoir #2

A biographer once asked Simone de Beauvoir if her romantic subjugation to Sartre in her personal life was at odds with her feminist theories. She said, "Well, I just don't give a damn. It's my life and I lived it the way I wanted. I am sorry to disappoint the feminists, but you can say it's too bad so many of them live only in theory instead of in real life. It's very messy in the real world."

Note that she is NOT:

    apologizing
    agonizing
    wasting energy trying to reconcile things that can't be reconciled

The Daybed

I visit a psychiatrist friend in her office while she is between patients.
The proportions here are soothing: old-world high ceilings, a sea green
velvet daybed, a faded Moroccan rug.

She is saying to me, "Your children may *look* from the outside like
they are thriving, but they may not be at all okay. When I was a kid, I
looked from the outside like I was thriving, but I was not okay. That
kind of deep damage doesn't always show right away."

She is making the argument that my romantic instability is taking
some sort of hidden toll on the children. The divorce. The two different fathers. The years of being on my own. That I have felt secure
because they look okay on the surface but I am deceiving myself.

My first response: to feel grateful to her for pointing out something
interesting and possibly important. Have I forgotten to worry about
the children?

Only later, on the subway home, do I start feeling anxious. The comment is worming its way in. And only even later, at night, do I start
feeling angry.

I did *not* say to her:

(1) Maybe in certain ways observing how complicated or imperfect life can be might make children more resilient or *more* okay than conventionally sheltered kids. Maybe the children of single mothers see their mothers as real people rather than cartoon cutout adults at an earlier age, and that early insight can help them later in life.

(2) Any kid could look like they were thriving on the surface and not be okay, even if their parents are happily married and raise them under the same roof.

Once when Leo was a baby, I asked her advice. Did she think it would be all right to leave him with the babysitter he has known his whole life for three days while I made a short work trip? She said, "Well, it would be better if you had a husband."

The kids seem okay, but am I missing something? Leo gets up early before school to work on his encyclopedia of mythological pests. Violet stays up late doing homework and goes out every spare minute on weekends to meet friends. But is there something destructive to them in the formlessness, the improvisation? My friend has trained in the best medical schools and hospitals for a decade. She is an expert; I am not.

The possibility of secret damage? The comment has a whole life span in my head.

My friend's parents had an eternally contentious divorce that has shadowed her whole life. As a result, she is a fervent believer in intact nuclear families. Anything else looks chaotic to her, pathological.

Only a couple of weeks later, at the Saturday afternoon meeting, when someone is talking about shame, do I realize that what I was feeling was shame. I am that well defended against shame; it doesn't announce itself or allow itself to be put into words. But that afternoon, what I felt when my psychiatrist friend alluded to my messy life damaging my children even though I thought they were fine was shame.

The Other Birth

When I was eight months pregnant, after things had deteriorated substantially, H. and I got into an argument. In an uncharacteristically
theatrical late-pregnancy moment, I threw the book I was reading at
the wall next to him.

He picked up the paperback and tore it into shreds. This shocked me.
It had an end-of-civilization feel. Who destroys books? I was about to
have a baby with a book destroyer. Of course, I had started it; I was
the one who had involved the book in the first place, but still. My
father had bought the book for me at one of the yard sales he scoured;
he knew I loved Graham Greene. It felt as though H. was tearing up
the book in front of my father, that my father was somehow now a
witness to what things had come to.

It did not seem auspicious that we were not on speaking terms so
close to the birth. I thought, if the baby arrives now, she will have two
parents who are not speaking. The next day, I went in to the hospital
for a routine sonogram. There was something wrong. The technician
said I needed to see the doctor. I asked her if she could tell me if the
baby was alive. She said I would have to wait and talk to the doctor.
I sat on a bench outside the doctor's office. In the hallway was a sign
saying NO CELL PHONES, so I didn't call H. or anyone else. I was
afraid if I stepped out to make a call I would miss the doctor, so I sat
there and waited for thirty-five minutes by myself, wondering if the

baby was alive. Finally, the doctor came out and gestured me into his office. He said the baby was alive but losing amniotic fluid and had to be delivered right away. Forty-five minutes later, just in time for H. to arrive from his office in rush-hour traffic, the baby was delivered by emergency caesarean. A four-and-a-half-pound preemie. Once we got to our room, a nurse said, "I've seen cats bigger than that baby."

In the maternity ward afterward, my heart was racing, my blood pressure skyrocketing. The doctors did a few blood tests for a post-pregnancy condition, preeclampsia, but they all came back negative. There seemed to be no medical reason my heart was beating so quickly. They moved me to a private room with the baby for a "magnesium treatment," which slowed things down. It was an awful feeling. A thick syrup running through my veins. A truck barreling through my head. It was impossible to stand or get up from the bed.

H. left for the office. My mother sat in the chair next to me all day. I know my mother was wondering why H. was not staying with us, but she didn't say anything.

The baby was in a clear plastic cart next to the bed. The hospital baby clothes were swimming on her. She was the only newborn on the ward with cheekbones. Her head was the size of an orange. I noticed that other people seemed a little wary of picking her up, but to me she looked beautiful. One of the nurses called her "Skinny Minnie."

Claude

My friend Claude does not go in for inhibitions of any kind. Nearing fifty, newly divorced, she sees in a magazine a top ten list of the city's most eligible bachelors and promptly emails number seven, asking him out.

Why shouldn't she email a stranger and ask him out? Why does it make me uncomfortable? I feel like she is exposing herself to some harshness in the world. Is the risk that she might look desperate? Who cares? Claude shows me photos of number seven, some kind of urban home decor entrepreneur, handsome, sandy hair, glasses, on a clear orange plastic chair. He looks nice enough, but I still think it's weird that she wrote to him because he is on a list of eligible bachelors.

A man, a doctor and writer, once called me on my office phone out of the blue when he liked something I wrote. Aside from the fact that no one actually calls me on my office phone, I did not find it that creepy or off-putting; in fact, after a brief correspondence, I agreed to meet him for a drink. The gesture seemed kind of bold (i.e., not *aggressive*, just sort of forcefully and exotically putting himself into the world) and flattering. If it's all right for him to ask out a total stranger, why not for Claude?

Claude does not feel shame, she does not apologize, she refuses to read a room. This could be bravery or originality, but for some reason she is entirely unworried about other people's judgments, about very high levels of self-exposure. I can see objectively that these are laudable traits. She is not insecure. She is not catering to other people's expectations or engaging in routine dishonesties and disingenuousness. She doesn't play games.

Another friend of mine says, "There is no softness to her."

As soon as she became single, she launched a quasimilitary campaign to find a man. She had five dating profiles and Tinder. She brings much younger men to dinner parties. I am impressed by her efficiency and resolve. If you ask her, she will say, "I want a partner. I want someone to do the dishes with." Why do I find the word "partner" so unappealing, so demoralizing? I guess I have mixed feelings about whether I want someone I can do the dishes with.

I never tried online dating. To admit that I was looking for someone, such a common and innocuous admission, would be hard for me to make, so hard that I am not, in fact, looking and am doing something more like waiting.

One night Claude meets a man she likes at a dinner party. He is someone who flirts. Afterward, under the streetlamps at midnight, she asks him if he wants to go somewhere. He tells her that he is not interested. A few weeks later she texts him that she is at party at a bar in his neighborhood. He is put off by this and tells her so. But she doesn't care. It's his problem, not hers. It was just a friendly text.

The man complains about this to me later. He finds it strange. It's a minor incident, but he didn't like the feeling of being pursued, of the tables being turned. Chris Kraus explored this territory in *I Love Dick*, a novel about a frustrated filmmaker who actively pursues a man named Dick, whom she barely knows; she turns that pursuit into an art project, a meditation on female desire. Dick says to the fictional Chris, "But you don't know me! We've had two or three evenings! Talked on the phone once or twice! And you project this shit all over me, you kidnap me, you stalk me, invade me with your games, and I don't want it! I never asked for it! I think you are evil and psychotic!"

Claude's friends laugh at her directness as a way of managing their discomfort. She pursues men in a matter-of-fact way. She is strangely honest, brisk. If she is hurt, she will say that she is hurt.

Her vulnerability awakens something savage in me, or something threatened. Her aggressive or adamant pursuit of her desires is dangerous to me somehow, imperiling something I am invested in. (What is this thing? My own containment of that vulnerability? My refusal of it?) To even call it aggressive is to collude, of course, but I can't help viewing it that way, even though I would like to.

Claude is unwilling to accept her place in the system. The system, seen from the outside, is flimsy, outdated. Nobody likes the system or thinks it is fair, but we accept its solidity, its existence; we have lived with it all of our lives; we intuit it when we can't see it, can feel its contours in the dark.

I feel protective of Claude but at the same time weirdly bothered by her need to be protected. I find myself gossiping about her with a man in my bed, analyzing from a distance. But I love Claude. There is something wrong in my eagerness to distance myself from her, to want to establish myself as safely and securely *not like her*. The reason must be not that I think she is different from me but that I think she is the same.

Ultimately, people like Claude, who are oblivious to the system or dare to ignore it, are challenging, particularly to those who feel oppressed by the system, have struggled within it and made their peace with it. Is it possible that through sheer force of will she can evade the system, break free? By not observing it, she renders it irrelevant and renders your own barely conscious bowing to it ridiculous or craven, which it so clearly is.

Find a way to make it your experimental art project and not his.

Maybe number seven is relieved when he gets Claude's email, maybe he finds it refreshing and bold and is, for a moment, intrigued as he drinks his iced almond milk latte on his Roche Bobois couch. In fact, he sees Claude one or two times before he retreats, reverts back to his place on the list, becomes untouchable again.

Lady/Lapdog

Reading *I Love Dick* unsettles me. I find it riveting but also sort of repulsive. A similar fascinated but sickened feeling rereading *Wuthering Heights* recently.

Here is the fictional character Chris having sex with Dick:

> I'm scared to talk and I'm wanting to sink down on you and then words come out, the way they do.
>
> "I want to be your lapdog."
>
> You're floating like you haven't really heard so I repeat it: "Will you let me be your lapdog?"
>
> "Okay," you say, "C'mere."
>
> And then you ease me, small and Pekinese, 'til my hands are braced above your shoulders. My hair's all over.
>
> "If you want to be my lapdog let me tell you what to do. Don't move," you say. "Be very quiet."

She is seizing an active role, in this pursuit, yet she is also dying to cast it off. *I want to be your lapdog. Small and Pekinese. Okay. C'mere. Don't move. Be very quiet.*

In *Sexual Politics*, Kate Millett established the idea that "sex has a frequently neglected political aspect." Through intricate close readings of colorful sex scenes by Great American Male Writers she pins down the aggression and domination fantasies at work. Kraus's lapdog scene is exactly the kind of passage Millett would have ripped apart; she skewers these sorts of sex scenes as "another form of compliance to masculine direction and prerogative"; in fact, she criticizes Norman Mailer for a female character being a "cocker spaniel" in one of his sex scenes. Only this lapdog scene is a woman writing about her own desires. In *I Love Dick*, the character has created this situation for herself. She is choosing.

Georgia

Georgia cooks dinner for her sometimes boyfriend, the father of her children. A Moroccan chicken tagine simmers on the stove, apricots, cinnamon, currants, couscous, a dinner that is a little bit nicer than what she would make for herself and the children alone. The strategy here is to seduce him away from his bachelor take-out life with the comfort of a family meal. If there were a perfume called "Home," she would wear it.

Her apartment is tiny but resolutely cheerful: a string of richly colored Tibetan pom-poms strung on the walls, red Marimekko duvets on the toddler beds. Her own bed is cordoned off from the living room with bookcases.

She tinkers with the tagine. It is possible she is stalling for time. The children, meanwhile, pitch a tent and live in the question: Is he or is he not part of their family? Is he with or not with their mother? The seat is empty, but he is always maybe about to arrive. The children are attuned to the state of anticipation, the exhaustion, the anxiety as their mother brushes a strand of hair out of her pretty face; she talks quickly, a little overanimated and lit up, as if she were on stage.

Outside is the lavishly starry night. The waiting doesn't quite end when the children are in their baths, even later, or wrapped in terry robes, or after they are asleep. It is always possible he will walk in, the configuration changing suddenly, opening up.

Of course I can be appalled the way everyone else is appalled. How can she? Why does she do this to herself? I understand her friends' frustration. How can she put herself in that position, and for so long, with such stamina? I am outraged and upset by the flagrant, almost unseemly subjugation, and yet how can I be?

If you pick a man this damaged, or you could say this unwilling, he will always be turning away. You will always be in a state of constant, anxious seduction. You will move through your days on high alert. That kind of attenuated awareness is itself almost sexual. The drama is narcotic. Why might this be appealing? Adrenaline. Rejection. Winning.

It occurs to me that this kind of relationship appeals to a highly competitive person, and Georgia is, in her own way, a highly competitive person.

Her friends will tell Georgia a million times that she should try to be with someone who is a little nicer to her, and she will always appear to agree, but she does not agree. When he wants her back, she will always go. When he invites her to move in, she will move in, with the children, getting rid of all of her furniture, until he tells her to move out a few months later. She will always be waiting. She will always be calculating how he would react to a job offer, to a joke, to a dress. Our words fall like raindrops. She is humoring us. She is thinking in her head, *but I love him.*

But what is the feeling you are chasing? Anger is energy. Not quite having is energy. Is it so surprising that Georgia is scarily competent at her job, that she will go into dangerous situations in faraway places?

That childish ardor for a love that demands sacrifices of you, the rigors and discipline of it, can look selfless from the outside, but it is not selfless. It is instead the elevation of a private fantasy that is ambitious and greedy enough to foist itself onto the unsuspecting world. That doesn't, for instance, worry about the two children sitting at the table waiting for the tagine, waiting for it to end.

Your need for him is stronger than his absence. In your glorious and enduring feelings, he is a bit player, almost irrelevant.

Secretly you are almost looking down on women in comfortable, in sleekly functional relationships, people whose husbands, say, take them out to dinner on their birthday. That kind of behavior seems almost vulgar, too obvious. The ease equals compromise. You are operating on a grander scale.

Sylvia Plath: "Everything I do with or for Ted has a celestial radiance, be it only ironing or cooking." There is a perverse power grab in certain forms of female martyrdom.

I remember when people would express qualms over my tenuous relationship with the Claw, when they encouraged me to end it. What they were saying made perfect sense. Of course I was looking for someone else, I would lie, but I wasn't looking for someone else. I was impersonating or counterfeiting a "healthiness" that I actually held in contempt. It was a little isolating or exhausting, this way of being, but there was a private thrill, like holding fireflies in a jar at dusk.

A point comes at the end of the night when Georgia finally spoons the leftover chicken into Tupperware, cleans off the oil that has spattered onto the stove, peers in at the children in a puddle of light from their rabbit night-light, and crawls into the bed behind her bookshelf, safe.

Simone de Beauvoir: "The day when it will be possible for the woman to love in her strength and not in her weakness, not to escape from herself but to find herself, not out of resignation but to affirm herself, love will become for her as for man the source of life and not a mortal danger."

The Walrus

At a party, I run into an old acquaintance who is now a successful painter, known for his wild Van Gogh–like self-portraits. He is wearing a purple tie and a weirdly shiny but beautiful black suit; he looks a little heavier than I remember, a mournfulness emanating off of him. He reminds me of a big, mournful walrus drawn by John Tenniel, the *Alice in Wonderland* illustrator, but attractive.

The party is in a sprawling mansion with many complicated terraces and marble statues and small hipster bands playing so casually and offhandedly it's like they just bumped into each other by chance with instruments.

There is an instant and powerful current between us, which is surprising because we have been seeing each other at parties since the nineties. I've always enjoyed his mix of old-fashioned gallantry and clotted intelligence and pure high-octane misery, but it wasn't attraction till now.

He tells me about being just out of a few weeks' stint at a mental hospital and the electric shock therapy, which scared him but worked.

At the end of the night, I stand on the sidewalk outside the mansion. He comes out a few seconds later and kind of walks into a kiss. We share a taxi home and say good night as I slip out onto the dark street.

He texts the next day: "If we stayed any longer in that taxi we would need a priest or a rabbi or a lawyer."

However, scheduling an actual time to see each other is labyrinthine for reasons I don't understand. He is from the Midwest. His language tends toward the regular guy, earnest, slow, down-home, among all these cynical, fast-talking New York people, he is genuine among the phonies, a Salingeresque innocent; that is his defensive stance, anyway, though it's tricky with his gift at it. "I've been exhausted and I want to sit alone in a room for a minute," he emails.

I make one comment that first night that we will be analyzing and cycling over for more than a year, that he will write many long texts about, many pages of email, even after we have otherwise stopped seeing each other and lost touch. Somewhere in the course of the evening, after Mary McCarthy–like volumes of drink, I appear to have said, in a context neither of us remembers, that he seems "dangerous." I have no idea why I said this. My best guess is that it was meaningless flirtation; it is, if anything, a compliment. Who doesn't want to be dangerous? He, however, reads it as an expression of my prejudice against the mentally ill. No matter how many times we go over this comment, we can never clear it up. In one of my early efforts I text, "Is anyone romantically drawn to safe men? I guess there are, but those people are, by now, safer than me."

He teaches at an art school once a week, on Tuesdays, but he can't go out the night before his class because he is busy preparing, and he can't go out the night of his class, because he has expended too much energy and is depleted, and he can't go out the day afterward because he is still recovering, so one three-hour workshop kills three days. Meanwhile, I teach seven and a half hours on Mondays and then come home to children who want things and talk.

Half an hour before we are finally supposed to meet in a restaurant, he cancels. It feels too awkward to cancel the babysitter, so I go on our date by myself. Bread with olive oil appears on a plate. A little glass carafe of wine. It feels decadent to eat alone. His ex-girlfriend's dog was sick. It is not surprising that this event demands an extra-oppressive amount of suffering from him, because every event demands an extraoppressive amount of suffering from him. There is nonetheless something glimmering about the way he describes this obligation; of course he is a gifted talker in general, so the words themselves are like flowers—you admire them and want to keep them in a vase on the mantle.

It seems a luxury, all this self-reflection, this elaborate spiritual delicacy in the face of life's minor demands. I recognize, though, that everything is a canvas for him, a painting in the making, every bird that innocently flies past on a wet day against slate-colored branches is ultimately about *him*, his ever-interesting and ever-changing internal climate. I also recognize that this is the illness, the world chronically asking too much of him, and also the art, his having a lot to say about it.

Meanwhile, the midwestern flatland in his voice belies any menace; it renders harmless anything that could be alarming. He projects a down-home modesty or humility that is, well, at best complex. The line between all right and not all right is fascinating, my eyes always on that line, on the tightrope of it, the always-about-to-be-lost balance.

Weeks later, when we finally see each other, we have oysters and wine in a bar in the middle of nowhere, which feels festive and strangely normal, after the Treaty of Versailles–level negotiations we went through to get here. We walk home through the warm, empty streets of corrugated metal warehouses, past the lit-up bodegas. I am wearing heels but don't mind.

"I think I could maybe be a good stepfather to your children," he announces once we are back in my house, standing by the crowded bookshelves in the hallway off the kitchen. I glance at a photo of the baby at one, dressed for Halloween in a velvet lion suit, blond hair haloing into a mane, and am alarmed.

He smokes on the steps of my garden. We look out at the globe lights strung by my neighbors, two of whom are openly and good-naturedly spying on us from their decks.

Once we are in my bedroom, he apologizes ahead of time for the little bit of weight that he gained in the institution. I murmur something reassuring. This bothers, in fact, actively offends him because it seems to be insulting or dismissing or somehow not properly valuing his real body, which is the one before he went in, and this one in front of me definitively isn't. This is confusing, as I do not want to say that he does look flabby, and in fact, in this moment, I am not in any way thinking that. There is, in other words, an added difficulty.

The sex is memorable. He crosses over in a way that more stable people don't really cross over. I am afraid of him in a way that makes me want to see him again.

In the weeks that follow, I feel like I could maybe make things a little better for him. Is there vanity here? Some idea of easing things, of transforming things, some latent maternal instinct to help or plan. This feeling of being radically needed or soothing or rescuing is appealing, though also, I guess, suspect when it's not in relation to your actual children. The potential dependency being nurtured is flattering, renders you irreplaceable, is less fickle and quicksilver than romantic love, more absolute and commanding. Everyone knows this, yet I continue to believe my motives to be good. Wanting to take care of him, to solve problems for him, to undo the damaging harm, to fix things so he is less vulnerable. Fantasies of quasimaternal power involve a tricky kind of subjugation to someone else's difficulties; it is an antique female idea of taking care of things, assuming control, but at the same time erasing one's own desires. I have a feeling he arouses this brisk maternal instinct in a lot of women, an army of brisk mothers who melt for him.

He is, however, developing an idea of me as brutal, cruel, which is confusing because from any outside angle it looks mostly like I am besotted by him and he kind of likes me but is too derailed by daily errands and sorrows to ever actually leave his house and see me.

The relationship ends abruptly at a party thrown by the same people who threw the one where we first met. Someone informs me that he is dating his twenty-one-year-old assistant, and he walks in with her. She is apple cheeked and I think wearing some kind of flouncy peasant skirt, though I am not entirely sure since I glimpse her for only a second before she is swallowed into the crowd. I leave the party, which is on the far West Side, in driving rain, trying to find a cab, even though there are no cabs. Through his usual ever-mesmerizing acrobatics he manages to transform the incident into something I or at least the ever-unfair universe has done to him. He texts me angrily later that night, "How could I know you would be at the party?"

A few weeks later, I hear that he is engaged to the assistant. He writes several dazzling but garbled and overlong texts about how what happened between us has nothing to do with anyone else.

A few months later, the engagement ends. He takes me out for champagne and oysters and says that she tried to take all of his money and that she was psychotic and a grifter. I admire his use of the word *grifter*.

Susan Sontag

Reading Susan Sontag's journals in a windowless archive in Los Angeles.

The bewildering discrepancy between her supreme confidence as a thinker and how she behaved in her romantic life, in which she often felt abject or desperate: "If I write, too, it will stop this uselessness of just sitting and staring at her and begging her to love me again. . . . It hurts then to love. It's like giving yourself to be flayed and knowing that at any moment the other person can just walk off with your skin"; "Hot waves of shame, and all that. I never had any illusion that she was in love with me, but I did assume she liked me."

How to connect the intellectual bravura, the almost grandiose sense of self, the astonishing will, with the role she played with some of her lovers? And yet there is also the joy of strong feeling that she clearly seeks out and craves. The feeling of romantic subjugation is another thing she will obtain for herself. What is the draw of a sometimes subjugation, the indescribable rogue need for it? This is what Simone de Beauvoir was talking about with the gap between theory and real life, the usually hidden moments when power and composure and outside self dissolve.

But what is the feeling you are chasing? Anger is energy. Not quite having is energy. Is it so surprising that Georgia is scarily competent at her job, that she will go into dangerous situations in faraway places?

That childish ardor for a love that demands sacrifices of you, the rigors and discipline of it, can look selfless from the outside, but it is not selfless. It is instead the elevation of a private fantasy that is ambitious and greedy enough to foist itself onto the unsuspecting world. That doesn't, for instance, worry about the two children sitting at the table waiting for the tagine, waiting for it to end.

Your need for him is stronger than his absence. In your glorious and enduring feelings, he is a bit player, almost irrelevant.

Secretly you are almost looking down on women in comfortable, in sleekly functional relationships, people whose husbands, say, take them out to dinner on their birthday. That kind of behavior seems almost vulgar, too obvious. The ease equals compromise. You are operating on a grander scale.

Sylvia Plath: "Everything I do with or for Ted has a celestial radiance, be it only ironing or cooking." There is a perverse power grab in certain forms of female martyrdom.

I remember when people would express qualms over my tenuous relationship with the Claw, when they encouraged me to end it. What they were saying made perfect sense. Of course I was looking for someone else, I would lie, but I wasn't looking for someone else. I was impersonating or counterfeiting a "healthiness" that I actually held in

Once my mother and I were taking a walk on the beach on a gray day and we saw a naked man emerge from the ocean in the thick fog. The man is like that man. Not quite of this world. My mother and I have to ask ourselves if we have imagined or conjured him.

I am also familiar with the particular logic by which pain becomes evidence of the extraordinariness of a love. How suffering slowly, subtly edges into being the point. The intensity of feeling is what matters and the anxiety surrounding it an almost pleasurable penumbra. Impossibility provokes, arouses. What could be more desirable than someone who is always there but not there?

Roland Barthes: "Isn't desire always the same whether the object is present or absent? Isn't the object *always* absent?"

I remember curling up with *Wuthering Heights* as a child. The craggy blankness of the moor. The sweetness of the separation. This is the bookish girl's happy ending: the pain itself. It would be too obvious to call it masochistic. It is that, but it is also wildly pure, uninvolved with the other person, independent of them. Unlike most romantic attachments, this one is private, free, inventive, ranging. The fantasy, untouched or unbothered by the nearness or constant presence of another person.

As an adult, I find Heathcliff's sadism less subtle, less *ambient* than I had remembered. He hangs Isabella's dog. He is trying to brutalize her, but she will not be brutalized. She loves him in spite of this, or one could say because of this. I had forgotten that scene.

when I have had a couple of extra drinks and am quite sane, that I realize how lucky I am. Saved, rescued, fished-up, half-drowned, out of the deep, dark river, dry clothes, hair shampooed and set. Nobody would know I had ever been in it. Except, of course, that there always remains something. Yes, there always remains something."

Although Sartre wanted to save the drowning woman, he did not want other, more ordinary things: say, to share an apartment or have more than a few dinners a week with her. Sartre wanted to save the drowning woman only sometimes . . . and only sort of. He did not want her to get any ideas.

The Boat Ride

When H. and I start living together, I forget to make money. Every now and then I write something and someone pays me, but it is his regular paycheck that covers our rent and bills. I don't notice or register this, even though before I met H. I somehow always remembered to make money.

Before they were married, a couple I know used to keep a list on their refrigerator: "L owes J $15 for dry cleaning. J owes L $20 for Indian food. L owes J $18 for wine." I was a little shocked by this list, by this keeping track. It seemed petty, foreboding of other more pernicious tallies and calculations down the line. If you are living with someone, why should it matter who picked up a bottle of wine for dinner? What is the deeper reason you are keeping track of these little debts, who owes whom? In my own life, I am much more comfortable with these sorts of transactions being erased or overlooked. I prefer not to think about them.

But was I wrong to lose track of this stuff?

The following minor incident will stay with me. Years later, I will write about it but gloss over the economics, almost deliberately missing its latent warnings, choosing not to see them, obscuring their destructive power.

In Cambodia, H. and I get stuck on an overcrowded boat in the middle of a giant lake in the smothering heat on our way to Phnom Penh. The water is the color of chocolate milk. The sun is insane. We should have flown, we should never have stepped into the unpromising boat, the dashboard covered in wires held together with duct tape. Before we got stuck, a mournful alarm sounded, which meant, we later learned, that we had run aground.

Hour three into being stuck: I am looking at the two sips of water remaining in the dusty bottle we bought in the floating village before we got on board, but H. remains calm. He is reading the *International Herald Tribune*. The Malaysian man next to me starts referring to H. as "moon man" and "man from the moon," because he is so unflustered it's not natural. This when he is not congratulating me on having such a tall husband.

Hour six: A rickety boat with a motor tied to it with string appears. Half of us get off of our boat to stand on it, the water pooling by our ankles, and it very slowly tugs the other boat. Eventually we can see a fringe of sugar palms against the flame colored sky. As we pull in, I develop a desire to stay at the nicest hotel in Phnom Penh. We never stay in places like this, but I am thinking of what it would be like to sleep in a room that does *not* have lizards crawling all over the wall like wallpaper. I am picturing fluffy robes and fresh-squeezed orange juice for breakfast. An incredible shower. I am feeling shaken.

In the taxi, I say, "Let's go to the Royal."

H. says, "Extravagant taste for a housewife."

I stare out the window. A rickshaw cycles past. A motorcycle with a man, a woman, and two kids on it.

Have I misheard him? I know he doesn't usually like hotels like this. I know he doesn't like spontaneous irresponsible expenditures. But is he really saying that I don't make enough money to suggest that we should splurge on a hotel room because we have had an exhausting day? I can't deny that there is a certain logic to this. He is the one paying for the trip. I have been spending months reading and taking notes for my book, while he goes into the office in a suit and bills clients by the quarter hour. Does he mean it, though? He is the one making money, he should decide where we stay.

I don't even care where we stay anymore. But I can't stop thinking about the maddening, intolerable situation. The ugliness of thinking this way. How did I get myself into an arrangement as antique and oppressive as this?

Jean Rhys: "When you take money directly from someone you love it becomes not money but a symbol."

The dependence is impossible. How have I let it happen? How has it happened without my even being aware of it happening?

I could say that I don't like to think about money, which is why this hasn't bothered me before, but not thinking about money is, of course, a luxury that someone is paying for. There is a cost to this obliviousness, this not thinking about money.

It turns out that H. was just kidding. He was not in fact calling me a "housewife." He was making a joke. He was referring to the fact that on my visa I had, as a friend advised, filled in my occupation as "housewife" instead of "journalist" to avoid any questions.

I am convinced that this conversation would never have happened in New York. He wouldn't have made the comment. I wouldn't have misunderstood it. At home, these arrangements are concealed, tactfully uncommented on. But we have been traveling in Cambodia and Vietnam for weeks; we have stayed in hotels with gold plaques on the reception desk that say NO CHILD SEX TOURISM, where we have nonetheless seen child sex tourism. We have gone to hotels and restaurants where we have seen countless Western men doing what Jean Rhys called "sugaring" countless Thai and Cambodian women. The million minor transactions usually hidden politely beneath the surface of relationships are out in the open here.

Virginia Woolf on economic independence: "What a change of temper a fixed income will bring about. . . . I need not hate any man; he cannot hurt me. I need not flatter any man; he has nothing to give me."

On the plane home, I tell myself that if we ever have a daughter, I will tell her, "Don't forget to make your own money."

When we get back, though, I start forgetting again.

The Writer's Wife

When I was twenty-five, I met a young British writer who was rapidly becoming well known. Famous novelists wrote rapturous reviews of his first book, which was translated into twelve languages. His face was in every newspaper and magazine I opened. He lived in London, and we sent each other hundreds of faxes, printed on delicate, slippery, see-through paper. We spent a week at his mother's house in Virginia, where I borrowed her beautiful bathing suits and he drove us to supermarkets on the wrong side of the road.

I was living in a one-room apartment where the pipes leaked, and I was lucky to have a nonexpired lemon yogurt and half a bottle of wine in my refrigerator, whereas he seemed to have a fully assembled adult life with a linen closet and a proper office. At dinner, I would drink wine and he would drink grapefruit juice, not because he was a recovering alcoholic but because he liked control and wanted to be clear-headed the next day for work.

We talked about my moving to London. I went so far as to talk to an American woman who moved to London for her husband, about what it was like. Underneath all this for me was the question: Could I manage being the wife of a famous writer? Watching people struggle to include me at a party, dutifully asking about the children as a way of bringing me into the conversation. I looked into that future. I had a premonition that if I stayed with him, I would stop writing so he could be the writer. I would leave the field so we wouldn't have to compete. This competing, even the sparring, fruitful intellectual kind we currently enjoyed, would ultimately be toxic. I could feel that already; we were staying up all night talking, but what exhausted us in a good way now would exhaust us in a bad way later. If he did have to compete with me, I intuited, he would ultimately have to leave me for someone wholly warm and nurturing, the traditional writer's wife. I didn't really blame him. I wanted a traditional writer's wife, too.

For a minute, though, I considered it: living in a London town house, being a late-night editor for his new pages, a good conversationalist over dinner after his long day of work, the erasing of myself. With him I would live a perfectly orderly, unstrained life. I could write a few little things, but those things wouldn't matter. The truth is, the idea wasn't unappealing. I felt a kind of secret thrill thinking of it. The pressure or burden of ambition being removed, handed to someone else. To recede. To give work up for connection, which is after all what matters when you die, not the books you are struggling to write or the sentences you are haggling over with an editor or the flickering connection to a single reader far away who may or may not care what you are saying anyway. To vicariously succeed, in the way women had for generations. To be taken care of. To stop wanting to be in "the world." The wanting was tiring. I could almost but not quite imagine it.

Right after I married H., I met the writer for lunch. We hadn't talked in a while. I told him I had married a lawyer. He said he could see himself marrying a doctor's daughter.

Robert Lowell wrote a letter to his friend Elizabeth Bishop saying that marriage to her was "the might have been for me, the one towering change, the other life that might have been had."

Looking back, of course, there is absolutely no logical reason it should have been a competition. We could have both been writers. The feeling that there was space for only one writer was irrational. I could have learned to deal with his success, to not feel eclipsed or overtaken by it. He could have tolerated my occasional bursts into print. But I think of a drawing D. H. Lawrence made for his wife, Frieda, in Capri. It is a picture of Jonah confronting the whale, with the caption "Who will swallow whom?" I was crazy about him, but it was that: *Who will swallow whom?*

Students

One day, by chance, over lunch, I learn the identity of the woman who called me and wouldn't give her name. Before she was the Claw's girlfriend, she was his student in London.

I think back to my favorite male students. I am often charmed or impressed by or protective of them, but I never want to sleep with them. They are not filed that way in my mind. How could I be attracted to them when I have so much power over them? I see their worried belief in their work. I muck around in their sentences.

I notice that for some (not all) of my male colleagues, that position of being in control, of being looked up to or listened to, of having someone drink in your ideas, your experience, your understanding of the world, is ambrosia. To pass along your worldview, to steer, to shape. It's not that I don't like that power. I may even revel in it, but it's just not wired in any way to physical attraction.

Sylvia Plath observed that teaching "seems to take much more out of the women than out of the men: probably the men get a certain physical satisfaction out of teaching the opposite sex." Their female peers, their contemporaries, their equals, will be critical, will already know the lines of a poem they are quoting, will not be inspired or imprinted by them in quite the same way.

Of course it is satisfying, feeling your ideas take. One day one of the former students I am close to writes, "I still use things I learned in your class every day." He lives in a different time zone. I follow his work from afar. I feel a rush of pride in him whenever I read something he writes. This feeling, like a superb moment in the classroom, is better than the feeling I get from writing, more narcotic.

So why do I care so much that the anonymous caller was a *student*? The idea of the Claw with a student depresses me. It diminishes him. I needed him to be rare, endangered, difficult to ensnare. The idea that he was so easily, so predictably won over, that he was, in the end, such low-hanging fruit, made him more ordinary. Even now, I go months without thinking of him, but I hate the idea that he could be ordinary.

There is more, though. The men I know. How many of them harbor secret longings for uncritical adoration? How many want to be looked up to? Inculcated with liberal politics though they are, how many of them secretly want the feeling of uncomplicated, untrammeled intellectual power over another person? Of admiration in its giddiest form? The professor, in other words, lecturing a student. The student who doesn't criticize or see the object clearly or put it into ten different perspectives.

There was a very quiet girl in college. She played violin and had a moon-shaped face, straight black hair, a shy smile. She did not seem particularly attractive or interesting to us, but boys were crazy about her. Was this because they could impose any fantasy on her? Years later a male friend explained the attraction to me and my friend Elodie.

"She *simmers*." We wanted to simmer too. He said that we were too "obvious." We put our personalities too aggressively into the world. We wanted the quiet girl's power. For years, we would turn to each other, only half joking: "Why can't we simmer?"

Simone de Beauvoir #3

S.d.B. wrote about the Independent Woman who does not have "the pure will to please":

> Her desire to seduce may be strong, but it has not penetrated into the marrow of her bones; as soon as she feels awkward, she gets fed up with her servility; she tries to take her revenge by playing the game with masculine weapons: she talks instead of listening, she flaunts clever ideas, unusual feelings; she contradicts her interlocutor instead of going along with him, she tries to outdo him.

Age Difference

A horrible rich person's dinner in a Fifth Avenue building. A table underneath a sort of rooftop gazebo. A uniformed black waiter bringing around a massive gold hunk of truffle and a shaver and waiting as each guest shaves gold flakes onto gluey risotto.

The women at the dinner are artfully plastic surgeried. They do not look their age, nor do they look precisely good or precisely young. They look instead like they have alighted from another planet, an alien species, bringing with them eerie and wistful traces of that other world.

This creates a little anxiety in the person looking at them, a hint of knowledge, a question you don't quite know you are asking. Their faces have a coddled, scared quality. A deer looking at you in the street, but a deer in a nightmare. A thoughtful plastic surgeon's idea of a pretty young woman, perhaps, after two martinis, or a painter's version, painting with the wrong hand, though with surprising adeptness.

A girl is texting at the table. At first, I think she must be the host's daughter. She has the long, straight, almost waist-length hair that is universally fashionable among teens. A child's drawing of a girl. The girlfriend, I realize later, of the son of a famous dead novelist.

A sad son in his late fifties. A pretty girl in her early twenties. The novelist, if he were here, would approve or not even notice.

When someone asks her a question, she looks up and answers politely. She is bringing out her nice manners.

The girl is texting because she is bored at this dinner. I would like to text, too, but it would be rude. Her age gives her cover.

What does it say about someone to have a girlfriend so young? The preening and somehow sad male vanity, the frantic insecurity, the doomed grab for virility and immortality? Yet we are scandalized or surprised by the older wife of the French president.

My date says, "Oh, come on, that's just the way things are. That's not going to change." His impatience unnerves me. As if I am refusing to accept a thunderstorm, an immutable truth. But I have faith that it's just a question of rhetoric, of persuasion, of clearing up a misunderstanding, at least, of the slow evolution into a view that better and more accurately reflects an equal culture. But maybe I am wrong and he is right.

D. once confessed that he didn't like being younger than me and unpublished. At a party, for example. He didn't want to be a plus one.

The Disciplined Collapsers

The Claw and I broke up over a line in an email.

He was already furious when I arrived in the restaurant, where we had agreed to discuss it, so furious that I was not sure how we would be able to sit in public, navigate menus, wineglasses, ordering, napkins.

The Claw's brutality is, on a good day, part of his allure. That he can dismantle my careful ideas of myself so easily and casually, that he has the will or intelligence to do so is irresistible; and yet under this always is the knowledge that he could go too far and will.

I used to resist the melodrama of Sylvia Plath's famous line "Every woman adores a Fascist," the driving absolutism, the too muchness of it, but that was pre-Claw. "The boot in the face, the brute/Brute heart of a brute like you." (Even now, I can hear the Claw: "God, you are really turning yourself into a cliché, not to mention me.")

Even in peaceful times, the Claw can be fiercely critical. To like him, you have to like the feeling of being elaborately picked apart. Why is this on any level appealing? Such a high level of scrutiny can be flattering. The appeal of being seen through in this way is the appeal of being *seen*. Most people don't bother. What was hard to resist with the Claw: the sweetness juxtaposed with harshness, flashes of tenderness against startling indifference. To be dissected by him is exquisitely wrenching because his indictments are so intricate; he is ferreting out your secret cowardice, your tender spots, your hypocrisies, so deftly, so intelligently, that in the end he can offer a benediction, a shred of approval, the faith that you are better than this, that you will be.

In this case, I have taken a splashy assignment that he sees as beneath me. I have taken it to pay the bills or, on a hazier level, to get other assignments to pay the bills. Worse, the article is a provocation: It will be widely circulated, vehemently attacked. It will detract attention from what I consider my "real" work. Yet I haven't resisted, never thought of resisting it. He is not, in other words, wrong.

What I wrote, though, in the offending email was this: "I was thinking there is almost a class divide between us, in that I have to write for a living, & have no other money: I can't afford some of the aesthetic positions you take. It's just a boring, practical difference between us."

I can't understand the rage of his response. It is clear that a red line has been crossed. I try, of course, to uncross it, to rescind it, or soften it or clarify it, but it is too late. He already hates me.

I think I hit something raw by dismantling this intellectual purity of his, by pointing to the comfortable legacy of his parents, the financial security underpinning his admirable independent thinking. I can't help noticing he likes taking people apart but does not like being taken apart himself: it's only *other people's* illusions that are fair game. But in the moment all I want to do is take back what I have said.

As we are talking in the bar, I am beginning to despair. I have pretty effective and convincing responses to what he is saying, but I am derailed by his tone. He is only meeting me as a formality. In his mind we have already broken up and he is already at home with his piles of books and papers, text messages from someone else coming through on his phone.

Yet things between us had never been better. We had come to a genuine equilibrium, or so it felt. His vanishing, my truly not minding his vanishing, my more effective and convincing suppression of any deeper feelings. What could he have discovered about me, after almost two years, in two lines of an email that changed his entire view of me forever?

His attack is frantic, unrelenting. He will not accept or see or register my surrender. I have dreaded and craved his judgments in basically equal parts, but this is different, more irrational, veering, wilder.

I can hear the Claw criticize even this: you are taking the easy way out, the worn and comfortable feminine position here, the wronged, the weak, the victimized, but you chose that, sought it out, played it up, cultivated it. The voice is right: I chose this, reveled in it, one could almost say escaped into it, vacationed in it, for a long time.

What happens next is slurred in my memory. I've had too many glasses of wine, as if after one more glass, the misunderstanding will be cleared up instead of becoming more out of control.

At some point, I walk out of the restaurant because I can no longer tolerate what he is saying. I am sitting on the sidewalk outside the bar at three in the morning. The drowning woman again. The street is dark, deserted. He comes out, and we argue some more and I can feel him physically containing his rage, there is an atmosphere of violence suddenly, anything can happen, and then he walks away from me very quickly. Not walking with me or saying good-bye or putting me into a cab. I watch him walking away.

It feels as though he is walking away from me so he won't kill me.

Elizabeth Hardwick, in a review of *The Second Sex*: "Any woman who has ever had her wrist twisted by a man recognizes a fact of nature as humbling as a cyclone to a frail tree branch. How can *anything* be more important than this?"

Even back in my room, at four a.m., it was not possible for me to leave the anger, to allow it to exist in the world. I can't give up his good opinion of me. The idea that somewhere on the globe he will be sitting at an outdoor table, ordering a red wine and thinking badly of me is intolerable, so I send him a conciliatory email.

I stay up all night and feel like death in the morning. The children are stirring. This is one of those times when it feels like the form my love for them takes is keeping up appearances. This is an effort in the desert of the next few weeks.

Alfred Hayes wrote in one of my favorite novels, *In Love*, "The only thing we haven't lost, I thought, is the ability to suffer. We are fine at suffering. But it's such noiseless suffering. We collapse, but in the most disciplined way. That's us. That's certainly us. The disciplined collapsers."

Edith Wharton

From photographs it is hard to see Morton Fullerton's allure: he is small, dark haired, olive skinned, with bright blue eyes, a mustache, a Victorian walking stick, a man evidently very involved with his own clothes; his friends call him "mysterious," "inscrutable." But there must have been something spectacularly attractive about him to both men and women.

Edith Wharton met him through Henry James, who was also quite taken with him. At first he was helping her place the French translation of *The House of Mirth.* She was in her late forties. The way she describes it is that she went out looking for friendship and found a kingdom. This was her first taste of sexual happiness. Her marriage was sexless and drab.

She was by this point a world-renowned novelist, a woman of independent means, the owner of a house in the Berkshires with fantastic gardens, a woman with several close, nourishing friendships with brilliant men, but she had not had this. Fullerton was a not very well thought of journalist at the Paris bureau of the London *Times* with money troubles. He was hoping to launch a freelance career.

The affair was erratic, fever pitched, on again off again. For her it was glorious, confusing, painful, enriching. While Wharton was experiencing this great love, he had other affairs, asked his cousin Katharine, who had been raised in his house as a sister, to marry him, only to later call it off, and was blackmailed by another mistress who had letters that provided evidence of his liaisons with men.

Shortly after meeting him, Wharton began a secret diary to record the experience. Is this a sign that she thought this love might be useful to her in her work, that there was something she needed in it? That she was working on getting it into words, gathering material? She often writes about "other women" who have fulfilling romantic lives. As if she had, for so long, been outside all that. She can use the longing in her writing, the sexual fixation.

In her diary she wrote in 1908, "I, who dominated life, stood aside from it so, how I am humbled, absorbed, without a shred of will or identity left; I am a little humbled, a little ashamed, to find how poor a thing I am, how the personality I had molded into such strong firm lines has crumbled to a pinch of ashes in this flame."

Ending a letter to him: "How I hate to stop talking to you! Good-bye—"

He vanishes. She writes, "Dear, won't you soon tell me the meaning of this silence." He reappears. Things cool and then resume. They are friends, and then they are more.

She writes, "I dreaded to be to you, *even for an instant*, the 'donna non più giovane' who clings and encumbers.'

"You knew why I sometimes draw back from your least touch. I am so afraid—*so afraid*—of seeming to expect more than you can give, &

of thus making my love for you less helpful to you, less what I wish it to be."

At times she seems to be writing the end to the story before it has come. She wants to turn the attachment into a close friendship, to take control of this turning.

> Nothing can take from it now, or diminish it in my eyes, save the discovery that what has set my whole being free may gradually, imperceptibly, have become a kind of irksome bondage to you. . . . It is impossible, in the nature of things, that our lives should run parallel much longer. . . . I know how unequal the exchange is between us, how little I have to give that a man like you can care for, & how ready I am, when the transition comes, to be again the good comrade you once found me.

In an essay on Wharton in *The New Yorker*, Jonathan Franzen called her letters to Fullerton "somewhat embarrassing." But they are madly articulate, finely written, terrifyingly observant, honest, self-reflective, rapturous, inventive; embarrassing only if a woman expressing strong feeling is embarrassing.

She is trying to reinvent or rewrite the situation so that it is tolerable for both of them. There is no point in judging: Is it healthy or not healthy, is it embarrassing or not embarrassing? It is a very imaginative person's way of accommodating an intense love for a difficult man.

She tries to construct a version of herself he can deal with: infinitely undemanding, flexible, supportive. She marshals all of her intellectual resources into making the situation okay so that it can continue, unsatisfying as it is. She does not want to lose him, even what little of him she has. Is that what Franzen finds embarrassing? Her honest assessment of the situation and her desire to stay in it anyway?

Her biographer R. W. B. Lewis writes that at first he thought she was "cool, even abrasive" and "puritanically repressed," but then, reading her diaries, letters, and unpublished fragments he found her humor, passion, voraciousness, her "almost unbelievable energy."

When her divorce comes through, she says: "I will eat the world leaf by leaf."

Franzen also found Wharton to be "lacking good looks and the feminine charms that might have accompanied them."

To Fullerton she wrote,

> Didn't you see how my heart *broke* with the thought that, had I been younger & prettier, everything might have been differ-ent—that we might have had together, at least for a short time, a life of exquisite collaborations—

> Sometimes I feel that I can't go on like this: from moments of such nearness, when the last shadow of separateness melts, back into a complete néant of silence, of not hearing, not knowing— being left to feel that I have been like a "course" served & cleared away!

One night, after things cooled, they have dinner with Henry James in the Charing Cross Hotel. They spend the night together in a hotel.

He sends her roses to the hotel the next day. After he leaves, she sits down to write the poem "Terminus," which both celebrates sexual connection and conveys its distinctive loneliness.

This was not a space Wharton was unequipped to understand. Before she met Fullerton, she had written *The House of Mirth*, one of the most profound explorations of romantic ambiguity of all time.

He tells her he is sick when he is not sick. She writes, "The one thing I cannot bear is the thought that I represent to you *the woman who has to be lied to*."

> What you wish, apparently, is to take of my life the inmost & uttermost that a woman—a woman like me—can give, for an hour, now and then, when it suits you; & when that hour is over, to leave me out of your mind & out of your life as a man leaves the companion who has afforded him a transient distraction. I think I am worth more than that, or worth, perhaps I had better say, something quite different.

She asks him at several points to return her letters, but he does not. He writes, "The letters survive. Everything survives."

In 1913, Fullerton published a political book called *Problems of Power*.

As Fullerton lay dying in his late eighties, his ex-wife, in her seventies, stormed into the house of the woman who was currently caring for him, also in her seventies, and demanded his letters at gunpoint. On his deathbed, he was still rousing violent emotions.

Wharton's biographer Hermione Lee points out that the affair's only lasting significance is "what Wharton made of the affair, and how it poured its way into poems, stories, novels, and those extraordinary letters which sound as if they have been written by the heroines of her novels."

In *The Age of Innocence*, Newland Archer says to the woman he is obsessed with, "Each time you happen to me all over again."

There is one revealing passage in the letters where Wharton makes her ambivalence about her own power crystal clear:

> There would have been the makings of an accomplished flirt in me, because my lucidity shows me each move of the game— but that, in the same instant, a reaction of contempt makes me sweep all the counters off the board & cry out:—"Take them all—I don't want to win—I want to lose everything to you!"

The gross inequity of their feelings was not a surprise or revelation to her. She saw who he was and still opened herself up to him:

> Dear, there was never a moment, from the very first, when I did not foresee such a thought on your part as the one we talked of today; there was never a moment, even when we were nearest, that I did not feel it was latent in your mind. And still I took what you gave me, & was glad, & was not afraid.

The Bug Box

H. arrives at the house with a present for Leo. It is a green-and-yellow-painted wooden "bug box" with breathing holes in it for catching bugs. He had it when he was a child. He stays for dinner, and we talk while we clear the plates and I put them into the dishwasher. The children wander off to get ready for bed, and we linger in the kitchen.

From the moment Leo is born, H. is sweet with him. When he starts to talk, Leo is unsure what to call H. His sister calls him "my dad." Leo starts calling him "My H."

H. takes Leo to the Bronx to visit a fire station where a friend of his is a fireman and lets Leo clamber up into a fire truck. He takes him to the country with Violet, and they swim in a lake and go blackberry picking and play laser tag and eat cactus salad in a Mexican restaurant. H. buys a special barber's kit because Leo won't let anyone else cut his hair. At two, after someone has combed his hair with a part after a bath, Leo looks in the mirror and announces proudly, "I look like H.!"

I have an image of Leo, home from college, going out to lunch with H. in Chinatown, asking his advice about summer jobs.

H. also makes one huge, incomprehensible generous gesture: he buys the other half of my house when we are in danger of being forced out.

He does not even own his own apartment and is profoundly averse to the kind of risks and commitments involved in buying real estate, but he does it anyway so that we won't have to move. I am bowled over by this.

One day we decide to go camping together, all four of us, in Pennsylvania. We load the tents and sleeping bags and bug spray into the back of the thirty-year-old diesel Mercedes. He has traded the blue one for a chocolate brown one, but it's the same car. I snap Leo into the car seat. On the drive, the radio is playing, and H. and Violet are singing along. At one point, we take a wrong turn and I am the one holding the phone with Google Maps, but H. doesn't get even a little annoyed. We are a happy family now that we're not a family. (*Isn't it weird?* a friend will ask later. It's hard to explain, but it's surprisingly unweird. It's like we have achieved the much-heralded comfort of decades of marriage, but it took breaking up to get there.)

We drive through Pennsylvania Dutch country, rolling green fields, silos, laundry strung out to dry on clotheslines. We drive past horses and buggies. Little girls with bonnets sitting in the back. A farm stand with Amish boys in suspenders and straw hats selling homemade root beer.

We stop and visit an Amish house with a farm, where we see a chick being hatched, and at night we sleep in our tents at the campsite. For breakfast, we go to a diner, with paper place mats with crayons and plastic-wrapped squares of butter, and I am aware that we look to the waitress like an ordinary intact family. I am finding this oddly pleasant and relaxing.

H. takes Leo for a swim in the river that runs past our campsite. Leo stands on a glistening rock in the dappled sun. It occurs to me that I don't know anyone who has an ex-husband who has stepped up the way H. has stepped up, who is as loyal, as involved, and full of love for not only his own child, but also for a child who is not his own.

At night, H and I go into our separate tents. The children are sleeping. Through the mesh window, I see couples sitting around fires on their folding chairs with beers, bottles of vodka, torn-open bags of marshmallows. The ground is hard under our sleeping bags, you can feel every pebble. I try to read a book with a flashlight. I text the Claw, but he doesn't reply.

In the morning, we go to an amusement park called Dutch Wonderland and ride on a water roller coaster. The ride takes an automatic photo: us four in a log, swept down the water chute, our mouths open, our hair blown back in the wind.

Photographs

I hate when anyone tries to take a picture of me. But when my book comes out, my publisher wants a photograph that they can put on the back flap.

Photographs bring out or reveal a fierceness I am not conscious or in control of; it's as if the camera strips right through the fun or good-natured or civilized or well-behaved layers of me and what is left is someone who has to kill her food with her own hands.

My friend Jason has already taken an author photo, but I look "mean." It's not just that I am not smiling but that I have what one of my former students refers to as my "death stare."

The minute he is not taking my picture, we are laughing, I am suddenly all the things I am supposed to be in the photo—warm! human! relatable!—but when he raises the camera to his face, it's gone. I am stony again.

I want to give him what he wants, what my publisher wants, what everyone wants, but it's as if another person slides between me and the camera. I can't get myself to look even neutral.

After two hours, Jason is getting annoyed. It seems so easy. But there is no softness, no suggestion of a smile, no warmth. Am I *trying* to be unlikable?

One journalist writes: "She seems infinitely more vulnerable in real life than she does in photographs, from which she tends to glower from beneath her long blonde curls, looking a bit like the MGM lion, seconds before the roar."

Some of this is shyness. I am self-conscious in front of the camera, uncomfortable. The rare outtake of smile is an accident. The glowering is protective coloring. The animal avoiding the predator.

Much earlier in my career, a journalist wrote that I didn't care about how I looked because I was not wearing makeup when I knew I was about to have a picture taken, but in truth I was a twenty-four-year-old graduate student and did not know how to wear makeup or even own any; for some reason I found the statement, and the picture that ran alongside it, strangely humiliating.

When my first book came out, a male journalist asked me in an interview, "What kind of underwear are you wearing?" A reporter for the London *Times* asked me, "How many men have you slept with?" Another newspaper in London ran a piece hinting that I was anorexic; I had ordered only coffee for breakfast during an interview just off the plane. I was shamed by the attention to the way I looked. It felt like my fault somehow, an exposure of a weakness, though the weakness may have been having any appearance at all. I had a sense of being judged on that image, of it obscuring or shadowing my work. It was impossible to argue with the image, to alter it. I couldn't control it like words on the page.

So why do these photos look like decisions, rather than failures or accidents?

Jason packs up the umbrella lights, his cameras, tripods, zipping them up on the floor. The next day he sends me an article on "resting bitch faces," or "rbf." The phrase itself, with its self-consciously interrogated sexism, its uniquely internetty way of self-consciously critiquing while simultaneously reinforcing a sexist idea, depresses me.

On other days I see Violet not smiling. She is very tall and serious looking. You need to smile more, I tell her.

The Dog

For some reason, Tim's dog moves in before he does. She is a Shiba Inu, bred to protect temples, and definitely cultivates the aura of sacred responsibilities beyond the scope of human understanding. Her name is Loup, French for "wolf," and she looks like a white wolf, aloof, silent. Once she killed a raccoon.

The children are happy to have a dog; in fact, they are happier to have a dog than to have Tim. The dog, meanwhile, sheds huge floating swaths of white fur everywhere. She chews our most beloved shoes. I feel like something is unloosed. The clouds of fur. The little bits of shoe on the orange Moroccan rug. Eventually she chews a hole through the rug itself, which is the first thing I bought for myself in my new house after leaving H. and therefore has almost ridiculous amounts of symbolic value, and is now basically ruined. I am not sure I can tolerate the disorder of the dog. I find myself not being able to. I sort of want to erase the dog, go back to the house the way it was before. Introducing a reading of a poem called "Spinster," Sylvia Plath calls the desire to keep control, to ward off men, "the neat disease."

One day H. is visiting and opens the door, and Loup darts out into the street and runs for blocks, dashing in front of cars, ignoring her name as we chase her calling it. She does not look back. She is like a dog in a children's book who is having an adventure, only this adventure is probably going to end under the wheels of a car. I have enough time to panic: If his dog dies, will we stay together? I also have time to realize how attached I am to the dog.

Tim

We meet on a blind date at a bar near my office. A friend had the idea that we should meet.

When I find him at the bar, he has long hair, a low scratchy voice, eyes the color of a lake in a storm, and a slightly confusing mien of expensive shabbiness. He feels strangely familiar to me, like we have known each other forever and played in the dunes on the beach as children, but also an insane electricity between us. On our next date, I go to his house, and he cooks veal and artichokes and burns his hand, and after that, we are together. There is no idea that we might not be together.

At first I am confused by this, and then I realize that what is confusing me is the lack of ambivalence. We just like each other. Everything is simple. No one is playing what people euphemistically like to call "games." I am disoriented by the straightforwardness. One morning, I randomly run into an acquaintance on Madison Avenue, leaving Tim's house, wearing a jacket of his that does not remotely fit, and I am so unusually, excessively happy to see this acquaintance that I realize I am happy.

We've both been living alone for a very long time. He tells me disastrous marriage stories, which, like all his most painful stories, are funny. We talk about how neither of us ever wants to get married again.

Tim, like the dog, is not a rules follower. He smokes two packs a day and has more tattoos than I can keep track of and tickets pile up on his car windshield because reading parking regulations or waking up to move the car would not occur to him. On one of our first dates he ordered in a hamburger for the dog because he had run out of dog food.

He eats Pop-Tarts, Dr Pepper, pizza, salted caramel ice cream sandwiches, ginger beer, grilled cheese sandwiches, fluffernutter sandwiches, bags of gummy candies. It's a child's dream of adulthood.

When he was seven or eight, he wanted to fly so badly that he jumped off a kitchen counter, madly flapping rigged-together cardboard wings, and cut open his chin, leaving a scar.

In adulthood, this flying takes more of an Icarus turn. He goes so catastrophically into debt for an idea— an art exhibit of Venice, California, artists in a fourteenth-century palazzo in Venice, Italy, with Andy Warhol's silver pillow balloons swaying in the wind and hand-painted gondolas and Courtney Love singing and an eighteen-piece symphony orchestra playing as Fellini's *Casanova* is projected silently against the palazzo facade—that he loses his house and his gallery and everything he has.

He is sober now. I did not know him in his wilder, out-of-control days. The stories surface every now and then, or hints of things, rumors of parties with strippers, or were they prostitutes?

A photograph someone sends me of him dancing on a table at her fortieth birthday party.

A photograph of a group of seventeen-year-olds standing in a circle with drinks in their hands, totally oblivious to Tim, stark naked, also holding a drink, the glow of a pool illuminating them. *Le Déjeuner sur l'herbe*, high school edition.

A photograph in a German newspaper of him in his thirties, running naked against the mirror painted with the menu in the restaurant Lucky Strike.

He spends a week making a Halloween costume for Leo, who for some reason has decided he wants to be a pharaoh. Tim spends hours cutting Styrofoam coolers and gluing them together and painting them gold to make a giant sarcophagus on wheels for the pharaoh to stand in. He finds a small gold body suit and gold sparkly Uggs and somehow crafts a pharoah's midnight blue striped headdress out of a bike helmet. I try to talk to him while he is working on it, but he can't hear me.

Another time, he stays up for whole nights making an entire Minecraft environment for Leo's seventh birthday party, which includes putting AstroTurf down on the entire living room floor to be Minecraft grass. Packages arrive every day with new materials. He prints out Minecraft skins and pastes them onto hundreds of small cardboard boxes that flood his office for a week, in order to build a Minecraft house the boys can walk inside of, and he makes a life-size skeleton horse and Minecraft torches for all of our walls. It's like a full-time job, this Minecraft environment. The day after the party, as we are walking to school, I ask Leo how he thinks the party went. He says, "It's kind of sad. In my whole life, I'll never have a party as incredible again."

Tim is one of those people who is better at making a world than living in the one we have.

Months pass; then a year. He paints the walls of the house lilac, peacock blue, midnight blue, cherry red; he puts up neon light sculptures made in the sixties by an artist from Los Angeles. I wait for calm or comfortable, but it never comes; I stay at infatuated, unsettled.

There is a strand of desperation between us I can't explain. It doesn't seem to fit into the conversations about whether we should make lamb for a dinner party or who is going to walk the dogs, but it persists under everything. No matter how long we are together, we never get to stability. We are always chasing it, coming close to it or losing it. I catch a glimpse of him sometimes in the house that we share and live in with our children and dogs and little paper lamps with legs that look like space aliens that we bought together, and I still somehow feel like he is someone I just met and can't quite have.

We are not talking or thinking about getting married. But then his mother says, after dinner on a family vacation, "So when is the date?" The candles flicker on half drunk piña coladas with paper umbrellas. "June," we say, looking at each other. "June."

The Rabbi

I had what I called a "relationship" with a thirtysomething rabbi we knew when I was fifteen. My friends and I were all enthralled by him, confessed our problems, made appointments, jostled and competed over him. He was tall, with black curly hair, caramel eyes. He was not at all "cute," as we would have put it. The allure was something else.

Jean Rhys had an affair with a decades-older man when she was fourteen: "Mostly he talked about me, me, me. . . . It was intoxicating, irresistible." Was that what I liked about him? I went to his office, and we talked about me, me, me.

The snow swirled outside his apartment. I had been babysitting his daughters. We sat on the pale blue Persian rug by the fire. He said, "My job is breaking down the normal barriers between people, and I've broken down the barriers between us." I cried when he said this and cried when he kissed me and cried on the snowy street when he put me into a taxi home and cried in the elevator up to my apartment and cried in my bed.

I was crying because of the abruptness of the change. It felt like *Alice's Adventures in Wonderland*: the sudden startling growth—first neck too long for head, then her crouching in a house because she has suddenly grown enormous; she is distorted by the violence of growing up, made monstrous. "Being so many sizes in a day is very confusing," she says to the caterpillar. This growing up is shocking, wild, unmanageable, also irresistible: *Drink me. Eat me.*

In the weeks that followed, I refused to go into his bedroom, because it felt like if I did, things would get out of hand. This was slightly overlooking how far things had already gotten out of hand on his living room couch.

He was also physically wrong-sized for me, too tall, too big. He tasted of cognac.

In her black exercise book, Jean Rhys wrote about her feelings toward the older man: "dreadfully attracted, dreadfully repelled."

I felt shame for liking the things we did, for wanting them. I felt a deep repulsion at what was happening even as I was enjoying it. There was a wrongness I couldn't shake. I hadn't gotten my period yet.

When we had sex, he used the phrase "make love," which sickened me and still sickens me. "You are the most powerful of all of them," he said to me. "One day they will notice." He meant the boys. He saw the boys my age not liking me.

He gave me a thick rubber band, which I wore around my wrist. We rode the subway to Coney Island, and when it rumbled above ground, daylight filling the car, I was suddenly nervous about how we looked to other people. We walked on the windy, deserted boardwalk and ate salty thick-ridged Nathan's French fries with lots of ketchup, and I felt the wrongness again.

It was fear but also disgust, a disgust I quickly aimed at myself, not him. He was peripheral or irrelevant to the disgust. The wrongness was a feeling of towering taboo, not exciting but sickening, adjacent to incest.

For some reason, I find myself cross-examining my fifteen-year-old self like a lawyer looking for inconsistencies in her testimony. She admits that she went to his house very late at night in a snowstorm with her best friend, Sara, and a bottle of cheap pink champagne. She admits that she was flirting with him. Both she and Sara were. On some level she wanted or provoked this response, she just didn't actually think she would get it. This sort of crush is meant to remain formless, to be free floating, to be unloosed as energy in the world, not acted on.

I try to put myself in his position, freshly divorced, shell shocked, a girl doing math homework barefoot on his couch, babysitting his daughters, appearing less challenging or provoking than some of the adult women in his orbit who judged him and wanted things.

Now that I understand more clearly what fifteen looks like to thirty-five, though, it's harder to wrap my mind around. I also wonder why he didn't pick one of my friends, who also hung around him, more experienced or voluptuous, closer approximations of women, better knock-offs. I was developmentally behind from a lung illness that had kept me in and out of the hospital for a year, and I looked years younger than I was. Was he actually a pedophile? Did he like that I was so conspicuously physically not ready?

In the weeks that followed, the excitement I used to feel talking to him was gone—that excitement had been entwined with his being untouchably and safely adult. His plummeting suddenly into my world made him uninteresting to me, strange.

After a few months, I told him I couldn't see him anymore. I was cruel and abrupt about it, though it's hard to imagine he had deep feelings for me. How can you take someone so young seriously enough to love them? So unformed and posing. Or maybe this is just me trying to impose rational standards on physical attraction.

He showed up a little down the street from my school on York Avenue, waiting for me, holding a bodega bouquet of red roses with white baby's breath, and I was beyond embarrassed (old man, clichéd flowers) at the prospect of someone I knew seeing him. He sent me a fifteen-page handwritten letter on yellow legal paper, which I found surprisingly poorly written.

Later, at college, I thought it might be a good idea to call him from one of the pay phones outside the freshman cafeteria, to inform him that I had not been traumatized. Why was it so important to me to tell him that? To my surprise, he was not relieved or grateful but aggrieved, almost whiny. "Of course you weren't traumatized! I was traumatized!" He told me he had lost his job because of my mother, which I had not known. He seemed to blame me for this, even though he had gotten another comparable job in another state.

To what degree was he in power, abusing power? To what degree was the fifteen-year-old me in control of the situation, the way I remember? I look back at the Mead composition notebooks I kept at the time. I remember writing very graphic passages about the sexual stuff, and now I want to see them.

When I open the notebook, the explicit parts are blacked out with a marker or sharpie. It is impossible to make out the words.

I don't remember doing this, but I know the marks are my own. They attest to a blacker feeling than I remember. The pages look ugly, scarred.

Jean Rhys wrote about her old man in her black exercise book: "What happened was that I forgot it. . . . I became very good at blotting things out, refusing to think about them."

In my twenties, I wrote a strange magazine article about this affair: "He may have had the power of experience, of knowing what it is like to have breakfast with someone you've slept with, but I had the power of youth, of being the forbidden object of desire, the injured party, and it was a power I quickly learned to use. If he was exploiting me in the traditional ways in which older men exploit young girls, I was exploiting him in the less well publicized ways in which young girls exploit older men."

To me, this sounded good on the page. I was not being dishonest, but I was still obscuring something with this talk, still blacking out some part of what happened. Even as I wrote, I was aware of something unruly I couldn't quite catch in words, something just beyond my reach.

What would he say in this courtroom I was continually constructing in my head? He would not be lying if he said I liked what he was doing. It *was* complicated: I felt a lot of conflicting things, and disgust was only one of them.

In my strange piece I went on, "I can't say that words like 'assault' or 'molestation' accurately capture the confusing range of my experience. I think we use these words to protect ourselves from the disturbing ambiguity of these entanglements, the troubling implications of our own precocity." This is true, as far as it goes. It's just that now I can see in this sleek formulation my own effort to wrangle power, to claim my active participation, to clamber for it. In other words, I would rather look at the "troubling implications of our own precocity" or "the disturbing ambiguity" than the overwhelmed feeling, the wrongness.

The things I was writing in my twenties were not lies, they were wishes. They were late-breaking attempts to control and tame the narrative; to wrestle it into a story of empowerment, not weakness.

In my fantasy of events, I am never quite a child, always a sort of protoadult operating, Salingeresque, in a corrupt world. This cannot be quite true, I realize, as I look now at fifteen-year-olds, their flagrant admixture of bravado and childhood: they are not children, but they are *not* not children, either.

I look at my daughter, fourteen, her friends, fifteen. They wander in packs, tall, ripped jeans, backpacks, sneakers, giggling, phones. The effect is of a different species, giraffes maybe.

Later I will talk about it at cocktail parties or tell men next to me in beds, but by then it is an adventure, an urban coming-of-age story: it recedes into a story of my rush to grow up rather than a man's rush for me to grow up. This kind of emotional work is effective, those faraway nights become what you make them in memory, they are substantially, maybe almost entirely, transfigured, but every now and then, I am caught by surprise. The not okayness catches me by surprise.

In my early thirties, I decide to write a novel about the relationship between the real Alice and Lewis Carroll. I am surprised by what I am writing about twelve-year-old Alice's response when thirtysomething Charles Dodgson crosses the line without actually touching her. The passage seems out of control, her response is violent, her distress too much. I don't like what I am writing, I resist it, but that's how it comes out. Why I am writing this?

I have so long and so passionately resisted the victim role because I was not *purely* a victim, not *purely* traumatized, but I am beginning to realize that this does not mean I was not also or very complexly those things. Because I was not *purely* powerless does not mean I was not facing a man who was twisting or distorting his power; it does not mean that the wrongness, the overwhelmed feeling was not there. I have been looking for purity, interrogating it, but this led me to lose sight of something very obvious: I liked what we were doing, but I wasn't ready. The wrongness was not an idea. The wrongness was physical. Something harsh and sharp rose up to protect me from any contact with the wrongness. Something harsh and sharp in me.

Can I admit even now that whatever else was going on, he had power over me and he misused that power? "The power I had over these women," the comedian Louis C.K. wrote in his open apology letter, "was that they admired me." The rabbi did not harm or traumatize or scar me in any traditional or straightforward sense, but the toughness I constructed for myself in response to him, *for* him, the jaded gamine

I evoked or brought into existence to meet him, who was preternaturally in control, prematurely poised and powerful, was a costly fiction. She was so convincing and charismatic and fun that for many years I and other people lost sight of the fact that she was not me.

How to Ride the Subway

My daughter is taller now than I am. She is five nine. She wears cutoff shorts and white sneakers with gold stars all over them. Even though she is fourteen, men start to follow her down the street, call to her from cars, talk to her as she is coming up the steps to our house. She writes an assignment for a class:

> Put your earphones in and be aware of surroundings. Stand alone, but close enough to people that you are not totally isolated. Move away from those creepy men who watch and talk about you, and make sure to adjust your shirt so it doesn't show any skin. Actually, put your sweatshirt on. That will help. And yes, you might want to switch cars when you feel uncomfortable. You're fine. Just don't make eye contact. Remember when the drunk man asked you to come over and sit next to him and how when you didn't, he cursed until you could leave the car, and think to yourself that it could be worse. Don't tell your mom about these men.

When she gets around to showing this to me, the obvious comes as a shock. The dawning of her power over men is simultaneous with her growing vulnerability; she experiences both, so violently, at once. She discovers her power to attract men as a burden, a danger. It arrives, already fraught.

Simone de Beauvoir describing this stage: "Men's gazes flatter and hurt her at the same time . . . she feels herself at risk in her alienated flesh."

Her power itself is a threat, so much of a threat she is already writing how-to guides on protecting yourself from it.

The line is razor thin: You have to be confident but not *too* confident. I've noticed girls her age say, "She is really feeling herself," about a girl who seems too exuberantly confident, too into herself. "She is really gassing herself." The irony of these phrases is a cover for an elaborate and variously articulated contempt. They are delineating a taboo for each other. At times, at that age, it almost feels like the secret police will come in the middle of the night and take you away if you are standing out in this way. If you are feeling yourself.

In *The Lonely Crowd*, David Riesman quotes an interview with a twelve-year-old girl:

> A: I like Superman better than the others because they can't do everything Superman can do. Batman can't fly and that is very important.
> Q: Would you like to be able to fly?
> A: I would like to be able to fly if everyone else did, but otherwise it would be kind of conspicuous.

Cigarettes

I hate the cigarette smoke. Tim says he smokes one pack a day, but it's more like two. He can't sit through a dinner because he is always calculating the interval until the time he can get up to smoke, which means I am always calculating it, too. When I am lounging around with friends, in their houses, I feel his impatience, it becomes mine; it feels as though the pleasurable long, drifting evenings of my entire life before him are over.

We have smoking on one floor of our house. A "smoking section." Friends who would never dream of smoking in their own houses come over and smoke in ours. They flee judgmental children and spouses and smoke. They bring battered packs of American Spirits and Marlboros. It's like a little zone of the house where everyone can do whatever they want. Sometimes the smoke hangs in the air, there are so many people smoking up there.

The smoke is something I have done to myself. I never asked him to quit. There are certain things you can't ask of someone else, and this feels like one of them. He has already given up martinis, cognac, tequila, wine, Vicodin. He is a person who needs a vice if there ever was one; he needs something even mildly illicit or disapproved of.

Still, I could have *not* lived with him. I could have said, "Let's wait and live together when you quit smoking."

Did I think, *He won't move in if I say he can't smoke?* Did I think he would leave? Did I think he would choose cigarettes and the freedom to indulge in self-destruction if he feels like it, over me?

It may be that I like him so much that I like his smoking. No, it's more that I am unable to separate or cordon off his smoking from the part of him I like, the outrageousness, the pushing to the edge, the making jokes out of what other people are thinking but would never dream of saying aloud or would never even permit themselves to think.

In the picture I have of him in my head he is holding a cigarette. I recognize that this is part of the problem.

We make little deals. He doesn't smoke in the bedroom, but the smell drifts. I open windows, but I feel like I am breathing smoke. My hair smells like smoke even when I go outside. I google "secondhand smoke" and think about the children, who also hate the smoke. Leo writes an essay at school about it. He is worried Tim will get cancer. He writes Tim a letter about how he should stop smoking.

Sometimes I shut the door to the bottom half of the house to pretend the top half doesn't exist.

One day after a week of being very sick in bed, too sick to get up and smoke outside the bedroom, he just stops. He isn't trying to quit, nor does he promise or announce or even exactly admit that he is quitting when I ask him; in fact, he says he isn't making any statements like that. He just never picks up a cigarette again.

Fire

The children, on the bottom floor, make it onto the street. Tim and I are stuck upstairs with the dogs, dark smoke billowing under our bedroom door. The flames lapping up the stairway walls. I lie awake sweating in terror. I smell the smoke. But there is no fire. I walk downstairs in the dark. Still no fire. I check all the fire detectors. I check the stove. I had woken up when I was a child with firemen in my room, pink and green elephants on the wallpaper. My sister, in her drug years, had set her mattress on fire. I seem to be coming unstuck in time, as Kurt Vonnegut put it.

In the Wednesday meeting, someone says that worrying is like praying for a bad outcome. Worrying is one of the ways that the "healthy" members of a family inflict judgment on the ones who are screwing up.

If you worry enough, the thinking goes, it won't happen. You can ward it off by worrying about it obsessively. You alone control the universe in this way. But really the worry is just eating your days.

The fascinated invocation of worst-case scenarios borders on prurience.

Al-Anon people always seem to be talking about taking a walk, but that is the idea: take a walk, feel the sun. Do not think about things that have already happened or might happen or haven't happened yet.

My mother's worry about my sister is the theater I grew up in. Her worry is both a moral imperative and a problem to be solved. The interlocutor will periodically punctuate, "It's not your fault." That is an important part of the performance.

It's irresistible, my mother's worrying, one of her artistic productions, her manifest seductions of the world. Her imagination is very potent. Her worries, very well and vividly fleshed out. She writes novels for a living, but these private worry fictions are among her best work. The critics would stand in awe of her worries, riveted.

How can I blame her? I have no idea what it is like to have an unusually gifted child who can't hold it together in school, who is admitted to a mental hospital for electric shock therapy, who sells her body for heroin, who contracts the AIDS virus in the late eighties but somehow manages to be one of the handful of people who make it to the years when treatments are available. There is a logic behind this worry, an abiding pain. But the habit is contagious.

Everything could so easily have been smoke: the dollhouse along with the all the tiny cakes and tiny milk cartons I saved up to buy at the dollhouse furniture store on Madison Avenue; the cats, Charlotte and Sunshine; the dogs, Moses and Oscar; the leather Trollope editions my father collected during the war; the tiger orange-striped drapes; the long kitchen counter where my father made bread, which we ate right out of the oven with melting butter. The fear lives in me, as if I am standing there watching the fire from the street. The charred husk of my childhood house. What could have happened. In a sense, everyone in this situation has too much imagination. Someone could have fruitfully told us: imagine less.

My mother tells a story about driving through the tunnel to New Jersey as a child with her mother, who was very anxious about tunnels. Her mother told her to watch the walls carefully for leaks.

She tells another story about being a child on an airplane from Miami and seeing flames coming out of the engine. Her mother was scared of flying so had taken a tranquilizer washed down with a couple of scotches and passed out; later she had to be taken off the plane in a wheelchair. My mother thought that she was the only person who knew the plane was on fire and would crash. She spent hours concentrating on keeping the plane in the air, as if she alone could control whether it could fly. Can you give up being in charge of impossible things?

Jean Rhys

Much of her fiction takes place in the wreckage of some man. In a concentrated state of loss.

The Jean Rhys character: smart, passive, adrift, running out of money, drinking Pernod by herself in a mostly deserted restaurant and then taking a Veronal to fall asleep in a garish third-rate hotel room. Her grief, baroque and hallucinatory.

She cries in a café where an American stranger has bought her a brandy and soda: "I lie awake, thinking about it, and about the money Sidonie lent me, and the way she said: 'I can't bear to see you like this.' Half-shutting her eyes and smiling the smile which means: 'She's getting to look old. She drinks.'"

Shabby, a little ravaged, forlorn, and yet also somehow alluring. The world she moves through, gorgeous and melancholy.

> "People turned and stared at her because she was walking so slowly in the pouring rain."

In *Good Morning, Midnight*, Sasha is in a seedy hotel room in Paris, pregnant. The father of the child has walked out after saying to her, "You don't know how to make love. You're too passive, you are lazy, you bore me. I have had enough of this. Good-bye." Three days later, without any warning, he strolls back into the room.

> "I'm very thirsty," he says. "Peel me an orange."
>
> Now is the time to say, "Peel it yourself," now is the time to say "Go to hell," now is the time to say, "I won't be treated like this." But much too strong—the room, the street, the thing in myself, oh much too strong . . . I peel the orange, put it on a plate and give it to him.
>
> He says, "I've got some money."

Rhys herself lived a life of radical dependence on men. She worked as a chorus girl, a nude model, a prostitute, a mannequin; she was "kept" by a wealthy man who continued to send her checks after they broke it off. She was, however, not very good at dependence on men. She attached herself to drifters, criminals, other people's husbands. Some friend was always getting her a room, arranging tickets. She had three husbands, two of whom went to jail, and assorted other love interests.

The Jean Rhys character is also: self-absorbed, self-pitying, overwrought, blotto.

Anna in *Voyage in the Dark* says, "You think I want more than I do. I only want to see you sometimes, but if I never see you again I'll die."

What is unusual is how wholly she gives herself over to these affairs, how she lets herself be ruined. It's the intensity, the lack of balance. It's the alcoholic's intensity.

Her characters are just outside of conventional life: "Marya thought: 'Oh lord! What a fool I am!' Her heart felt as if it were being pinched between somebody's fingers. Cocktails, the ridiculous rabbits on the wallpaper. All the fun and sweetness of life hurt so abominably when it was always just out of your reach."

In Paris, Rhys got entangled in a painful triangle with the writer Ford Madox Ford and the painter Stella Bowen, whom he referred to as his wife. According to Bowen, Rhys arrived on their doorstep with a single cardboard box containing everything she owned. Bowen gave her a bed in their studio in Montparnasse and took her in. The couple took her to dinners, parties, restaurants, fed her, bought her drinks, introduced her to their friends. When the situation became too tense, Ford got Rhys a room nearby. He dressed quickly after sex, and she could feel him wanting to leave. In her fictional version, *Quartet*: "Supposing she asked him, next time she saw him: 'Heidler, save me. I am afraid. Save me.' Just like that." And: "Then as she stared back at him she felt a great longing to put her head on his knees and shut her eyes. To stop thinking. Stop the little wheels in her head that worked incessantly. To give in and have a little peace. The unutterably sweet peace of giving in."

Stella Bowen wrote of this period, "Here I was cast for the role of the fortunate wife who held all the cards, and the girl for that of the poor, brave and desperate beggar who was doomed to be let down by the bourgeoisie. I learned what a powerful weapon lies in weakness and pathos and how strong is the position of the person who has nothing to lose, and I simply hated my role."

In her eighties, Rhys says to the writer David Plante, "I don't dislike women exactly but I don't trust them." She also asks him to buy her a bottle of vermouth and complains that the hotel puts too much ice in her drink.

On another day she says to him: "My life has been turbulent and very boring."

I have a friend in real life who also lives in Paris. She says that she lost all of the hair on her body because of the shock of a relationship ending. She got pregnant by a waiter on a Greek island when she was writing a book in the café where he worked, and he left her when the baby was born because the baby had Down syndrome. She wrote in that book, *The Vindication of Love*: "I have been derailed by love, hospitalized for love, flung around five continents, shaken, overjoyed, inspired and unsettled by love."

When she was very young, Rhys planned to write a novel called *Wedding in the Carib Quarter* but never got around to it. In the notes for it she wrote, "No playing around with ME."

David Plante asks her: "When you dictate a sentence to me, I study it and think it should be banal and sentimental, and it's in fact, original and tough. Why is that?"

Money

Why is my male colleague, who has not yet published a book, paid substantially more than me? He says that when he originally got his job offer from the university, he negotiated a higher salary. When I was offered my job, I was so bowled over with gratitude that it would never in a million years have occurred to me to ask for more money. That would have felt rude or ungracious. I ask around a little more and find that other male colleagues hired at around the same time are also being paid way more than me and that they also haggled for extras such as faculty apartments or faculty apartments on higher floors with better views.

I am afraid to approach the chairman of my department: I worry that she won't like me. But of course, this was the problem in the first place. I tell myself it is absurd. The odd thing is, when I finally breach the subject, I sense that she does like me less. I can feel her disliking me in the conversation in her book-cluttered office, mug of tea on her desk. We have always gotten along well and I admire her, but she seems suddenly prickly, aloof, distracted by something she needs to get back to. Is this just because I have caused more work for her? Is it even true, or am I hallucinating it? Maybe she doesn't dislike me at all.

While I am worrying about this, she says, "You really shouldn't compare your salary to other people's." But why not? How else can you tell if you are being paid fairly? I am not sure what to say.

At around the same time, a female friend decides to ask for more money at her own job. She looks up a template of a letter on the internet and copies and pastes it. But she is a professional writer. Surely, it occurs to her later, she could have concocted a more potent letter on her own. Why she didn't think of this before it was too late? By using a template, she wasn't quite the one asking. She distanced herself. Her request was denied.

In any event, I have started forcing myself to ask even though I hate doing it. To an editor at a newspaper: "I would love to do this, but not sure I can afford to take the time to do it properly for that amount of money. . . . I am sorry! I would like to be more high-minded, but life intrudes. Is there any way you could do a little better on the fee?" I am not exactly presenting an Amazonian front. I am still, for instance, apologizing. I am a little shocked when she writes back quickly with a higher offer. I have stumbled on the keys to a hidden door.

Later, someone I am hiring to teach a course for my program asks me for more money. She apologizes, elaborately explains, contextualizes, profusely understands if it's not possible. Her email is like a little cathedral of justification. It reminds me of my own emails. I feel her anxiety, which is exactly the same as my anxiety in the same situation, a wanting to be liked, a cocktail party mentality in the middle of a business negotiation.

Of course, I don't blame her. To me, her asking for more money seems a normal thing to do. All the energy I have spent over the years appeasing, disarming imaginary resentment. Such a colossal waste of resources. All that energy I could have spent on other things. But the next time I ask, it will seem impossible again. I will begin work on my own little cathedral. "I'm sorry to ask this. I totally understand if it's not possible . . ."

Bullies

The higher-up person in my office who bullied me was a woman. When she approved of you, she could be warm and charming with a crackly laugh. She always sat with her feet up on a chair or on the table, which gave her an imperious childlike aspect.

One day, looking up from something on her desk, she tells me to photocopy something for her. Tells, not asks. Not in a casual, friendly tone but with a note of command in her voice, almost as if she is daring me to refuse. I know that she is trying to humiliate me but also know that I can't resist or say no because I am up for tenure, and that tenure relies heavily on her approval of me since she works with me more closely than anyone else. Am I imagining this? I don't think so. I feel her openly relishing the moment. I take the pages in her hand and walk downstairs to the copy machine. Her messaging is effective. I stand in the closet-sized room, and, from every angle, I confront the immense gleaming power she has over me. She can tell me to do something we both know to be outside the realm of acceptability in our workplace, and I will submit without question. She could tell me to organize her closet or pick up her dry cleaning, and I would do that, too.

While she was away, I briefly assumed her duties. Once when a graduate assistant emailed both of us with a minor question, she put my email address before hers. My colleague got annoyed and told me that in all future communications her email address should always be first. I half-admired her dogged devotion to protocol. She cared about whose email address came first on a random administrative email.

One day she offered to read my personal statement for me. This was a very long document I had prepared for my third-year review, an academic ritual in which your performance is formally evaluated by your colleagues; if they approve, you are allowed to continue on in your job. I sent my personal statement, and she had no comments or suggestions, which I worried was a little strange. Did she hate it? Had I written something beyond the pale? A few days later, one of my colleagues called to tell me that she was trying to mobilize people before the meeting to get me fired.

During this time, I was pregnant with Leo and completely on my own. I started to panic about what I would do if I lost my job and my medical insurance.

At the meeting, my colleague had told people I hadn't done a particular piece of work she had asked me to do. Afterward, a senior colleague advised me to take a large stack of printed emails I had, proving I had not flaked out on that particular piece of work, and show the emails to my colleagues in their offices one by one, which I did. One of them said, "I don't like her, and I don't like you, but I knew she was lying."

There was a heat to my colleague's feelings that I didn't understand. I couldn't figure out why she turned against me. "Your problem," another friend in my department said, "is that you were surprised. Anyone else would have known this was coming."

At one point later, she and I spoke on the phone. I was questioning the fairness of her giving a class I had invented and developed to an outside person to teach when I was there, already on the faculty, ready to teach it. She said coolly, "A junior professor can't speak to a tenured professor that way." It seemed almost comic that she would actually put that thought into words, as if I were suddenly a kitchen maid who had spoken back to the assistant housekeeper on an English country estate in the nineteenth century. The hierarchies were that unbreachable. But again there was nothing I could say.

There was a male colleague around this time who would see me in the hall and say things like "Here comes Katie Roiphe with her long legs." I did sort of think to myself, now that's not something you are supposed to say to your junior colleagues, but it seemed harmless enough. It never menaced me the way my female colleague's machinations did. It didn't get inside my head.

At the final promotion meeting, where my tenure would be decided, she read a long and colorful list, filibuster style, of bad things that had been written about my work. This is not normally done. I don't know exactly what she quoted, but it could have been something like this: "Women everywhere turned on her with a ferocity spectacular to behold. No one, it seemed, liked Katie, and no one liked her book" (*The Guardian*). "At times verges on the arrogant" (*The Independent*). "A careless and irresponsible performance, poorly argued and full of misrepresentations, slapdash research, and gossip" (*The New Yorker*). "Intemperate attack on feminism by a student writing in a popular vein"; "a fictional creation that serves her rhetorical ends" (*The Yale Law Journal*).

While this was happening, I was having a very jittery breakfast across the street from the office with two of my junior colleagues, also up for tenure. Through the restaurant window, we watched the entrance to see if the professors in the meeting were leaving. But the meeting dragged on for almost three hours. We agreed that the meeting was going too long, and even my friends admitted this wasn't the best sign. Finally we saw a couple of professors from our department spill out onto the street. They were smiling and laughing, but that could mean anything. Were they yeses or nos? We weren't sure. Finally, the chairman called me. I went upstairs to her office. The vote had gone my way.

Eventually, while she remained in the department, my colleague would resign from her leadership role and the chairman of our department would offer me that job. It felt like a coup d'état I hadn't known I was staging. In the years that followed, I was promoted to full professor. She was friendly to me after that.

More Bad Things About Me in Print

I don't know what exactly she quoted because I wasn't in the meeting, but there was a lot to choose from.

"Perhaps this is why she seems so uptight" and "This summer, Katie-haters everywhere will be thrilled to hear, she starts work on a new book. She smoothes the retro mini-dress in an action that makes me think—who knows why?—of a butcher preparing to tenderise a steak" (*The Guardian*). "It's clear that Roiphe is, as she has always been, an embodiment of a particular kind of irritant" and "[I] once refused to shake her hand, 10 years ago, when I was working in an office where she came in for a meeting. When I told her this, she looked only mildly surprised" (*Salon*). "When I think of Roiphe back then, I think of a writer people hated because it was the thing to do; branding her as the *enemy* (of feminism, of cultural criticism, of the New York media scene, of whatever) was part of the rules of discussion" (*Los Angeles Review of Books*). "Katie Roiphe Is Big Immature Baby" and "Shut Up, Katie Roiphe" (*Gawker*). "So some of you may have seen Katie Roiphe's long and sometimes-sharp-and-other-times-kind-of-annoying piece. . . . It is so awesome to have one's work taken seriously" (*The Rumpus*). "Within a certain social circle—O.K., mine—mention of the name Katie Roiphe inspires exasperated eye rolls, forehead slaps, even hisses" and "Katie haters will be sorry to hear that it is very absorbing. The author has done something constructive, for a change, with her contempt for the contemporary age's lily-livered female psyche" (*New York Observer*). "A self-proclaimed bad girl and sexual rebel" and "It may be that Roiphe's friends have nothing to tell her. Or it may be that they have nothing to tell *her*" (*The New Yorker*). "Narrative may be a fine tool for placing others under the microscope, but Roiphe is noticeably squeamish about using it on herself" (*The Yale Law Journal*). "A mean girl in the cafeteria" (*Salon*).

Janet Malcolm

My admiration for Janet Malcolm is enormous, unmanageable. When she agrees to let me interview her for *The Paris Review*, I am terrified. No other living writer could inspire this fear in me.

She had agreed on the condition that we conduct the interview only in writing. She wants me to send my questions by email. She is not comfortable with the surrender of control implied by someone recording a free-ranging conversation. She is not used to being the interview subject, she prefers to remain the writer. Sometimes, if she doesn't like the way a question is phrased, she suggests a change, which I, of course, quickly take. She prefers to call the interview "a conversation," which it becomes.

After we finish, the junior editor we were working with wants to edit my questions down into actual questions. He wants them to be much shorter and resemble the way the magazine has been doing these interviews since before he and I were born. But that is not quite the spirit of what we had done. I was happy to whittle my questions down to almost nothing. In my mind, I was being practical. I wanted the piece to be published. I was aware that the magazine had tried twice and failed to do a Janet Malcolm interview, and I didn't want mine to be the third failed Janet Malcolm interview.

But Janet stood up for my questions. She didn't understand why I was willing to let the editor push me around.

She protects my questions and keeps them as they are. She says she will pull the interview if the editors try to change the format. There is no doubt in anyone's mind that she means it. I admire her intransigence.

I am not sure why I am so ready to chop up my questions. For some reason my questions don't matter to me, only her answers matter.

Once that's all settled, I sit down to write an introduction. After it's finished, I read it aloud to her on the phone from my office, which is a terrifying experience. I stare at the brick wall behind my desk. She makes one or two small comments but then approves it. Her tone is so opaque that I don't know if she likes it. I worry that she doesn't like it. I would not think of writing the introduction without her reading and approving it, even though this is not *Paris Review* convention. There is no element of this interview that is not under her absolute control.

In the interview, we talk about being a woman writer at the time she began writing. *The New Yorker* gave her a home decor column before she developed her distinctive style and came into her own.

> Women who came of age at the time that I did developed aggressive ways to attract the notice of the superior males. The habit of attention getting stays with you. . . . Here is another thing: during my four years of college I didn't study with a single woman professor. There weren't any, as far as I know.

Then she quoted Virginia Woolf's writing about feeling at ease with gay men. Woolf explains that the feeling of being with gay men has one drawback: "One can't, as nurses say, show off. Something is always suppressed, held down. Yet this showing off, which is not copulating, necessarily, nor altogether being in love, is one of the great delights, one of the chief necessities of life."

> Showing off to straight men remained a delight and necessity to women of my generation. Those of us who wrote, wrote for men and showed off to them. Our writing had a certain note. I'm not sure I can describe it, but I can hear it.

I try to go deeper into this. *What is this note?* It seems important. I feel like I have to know what she means. But Janet writes back, "Maybe we should move on to a new subject."

I want to write back and say, wait, let's stay on this subject! But I know I can't press her on it. There will be no mind changing. There will be no detours.

The thing is, I love the interview. I look insanely forward to her answers in my email. Nothing else I am doing grabs me the way this does. When I think for a moment she is going to pull out of it, I am devastated. For some reason the Claw gets annoyed by this. "Why do you care so much about it?" he asks. "It's just an interview."

Later a poet, Dan Chiasson, publishes a villanelle about the interview in *Harper's*:

> That day my objectivity danced with hers,
> Our journalistic egos danced a tango,
> And she rewrote my questions she had answered.

She'd interviewed herself, I realized later;
I was bystander to a rendezvous.

In the photograph that runs with the interview she is pretty and young, stretched out on her stomach in a bed, with an Audrey Hepburn haircut, in all black, holding a Siamese cat, and reading the Marquis de Sade. The caption reads, "Janet Malcolm with cat and Marquis de Sade, 1954."

The Wedding

My friend Osman, who is a fashion designer, made me the dress. He drew it on a napkin in a pub in London on a rainy night, but a week before the wedding it still hadn't arrived. Will I have a dress? I wondered. When it finally came, it was exactly what I had been wanting, the kind of dress you see on a Greek marble statue who is missing a head.

We get married at the villa in Jamaica where Ian Fleming wrote the James Bond novels, with a few close friends and our families. I carry orange and purple tropical flowers, and Violet and Tim's daughter are barefoot. Leo, in a blue seersucker jacket and shorts, carries the rings. Tim wears an arrowhead around his neck.

Little paper lanterns hang from the trees. The guests drink rum, champagne. The men take off their jackets in the heat. We eat curries at a long table next to the ocean as it gets dark.

There is an element of surprise in late weddings, especially in our case, since both of us might have seemed unmarriageable or, you could say, marriage averse. In my mind I have been thinking of marriage as surrender. Is there something good about surrendering? Of course, James Bond is the opposite of settling down, the opposite of growing up. In the corner of the main house is the desk where Ian Fleming wrote the novels. There is a glass coffee table on a base made of a naked woman on all fours carved out of mahogany.

The day before the wedding, I picked up one of the old paperbacks lying around, *The Spy Who Loved Me*, which turns out to be the only James Bond novel written from a woman's point of view. It contains the immortal line "Now don't hang on my gun arm, there's a good girl." Bond says this to Vivienne after she says she can't live without him. At the end, after he has left, an old cop explains to her that she shouldn't be in love with Bond, that there is no difference between Bond and the villains trying to shoot at them: they all come from the same "private jungle."

My mother, in reading glasses, gives a toast at the end of the long table. She mentions that a week after meeting him I said to her, I think this is it. Embarrassing but true.

While the band plays, Leo floats in the pool for hours. Violet sits on a stone wall with her cousins. Emily, in a red bikini top, is dancing barefoot, holding up her floor-length red polka-dot silk skirt. At the end of the night the singer wanders into the pool in her clothes. We jump in, too, along with the guests.

I like the mosquito netting around the beds, the huge rubbery leaves, the sound of cicadas. We stuck with the old vows: "With my body I thee worship."

Lucia

In graduate school I had a friend named Lucia in Comp Lit. She was short, pretty, a little stocky, with red hair, green eyes; at night she wore crop tops and tight strappy things in slight violation of the I-don't-care graduate student dress code. Her parents owned a Italian restaurant in Bay Ridge. She was an academic star; she won prizes. Her parents, she once told me, would have preferred she were married to all of this education.

Once she liked a man and showed up at his house naked under a trench coat. He slept with her and then, shortly afterward, found her too much.

She had a very brief entanglement with a handsome architecture graduate student, which in her mind bloomed into a complex full-blown relationship. In her mind, it had many acts. She threw herself into the relationship without his actual participation. She had some sort of erotomania; nothing he could do or say or *not* do or say could impinge, even slightly, on her fantasy world.

For him it was a couple of brief, meaningless encounters, except that she wouldn't let it go. He went ahead with his life, speaking to her rarely, getting a girlfriend, pursuing his work. She, meanwhile, acted as if they were in a relationship, and this acting was so convincing that when we were with her we almost forgot the truth. She would analyze

small things he had said to her, like a book recommendation or a
comment like "Aren't you freezing?" so minutely that we had trouble
remembering the whole elaborate framework was pure invention. It
seemed impossible someone could construct such a detailed psycho-
logically nuanced analysis on the foundation of literally nothing.

In conversation we were in a strange place. It was not possible to
puncture her idea of what was happening, so we found ourselves
talking about the fictional situation, listening sympathetically, even
offering advice, though that advice was usually in the direction of
forgetting about him and moving on. For some reason we never said
to her, "But you barely know him!" or "All of this is in your head."
There were times when we found ourselves almost wanting to believe
her. Her investment in the facts was always more powerful than ours.

One night in the only bar in town, where we all, somewhat unhealth-
ily, saw each other every night, she poured a drink on his head. On
another, she threatened his new girlfriend with a knife. It was her
understanding that he was cheating on her with this woman. I think
it was a butter knife or some sort of very nonthreatening knife, but
it was nonetheless a scandal in our tiny, otherwise staid community.

The whole increasingly disturbing affair culminated in a night, when
she wrote to him that she was pregnant with his child. This was not, to
our knowledge, true, though in her mind, I think it was, and her fury
at his betrayal was intense. He was cheating on her. She was pregnant.
If only he could see and acknowledge their magnificent connection.
In order to make a point, she broke into the studio where the archi-
tects worked, a beautiful glass building, at night and decorated his
area of the studio with baby toys. When he walked in the next day, his

drafting table was strewn with pacifiers and little bears and bottles and rattles. They were hanging everywhere.

It was mesmerizing to watch desire freed from an unsatisfying man, unloosed and on its own. The crazy desperate need for a man that could basically supersede the physical world. It was strange to witness the power of the fantasizing, the will to make the world into what you wanted it to be, to impose, to create from scratch a love. To live your one side of it.

It could almost have been a piece of feminist performance art, though it was also sad.

Eventually the university took some sort of disciplinary action, I can't remember precisely what, and she sought some sort of treatment and recovered, or at least I think she recovered.

A while ago, I tried to figure out what had happened to her. After some searching online, a single photo of her appeared: still pretty but brisker, busier, with short hair, in a suit, very pulled together, professional, an ID hanging around her neck, walking next to the French ambassador. It seemed very possible that this whole affair could have been one insane isolated storm in her past, since blurring into the crazy things we all do when we are young.

Rebecca West: "Since men don't love us nearly as much as we love them that leaves them a lot more spare vitality to be wonderful with."

Dark Thing

I often have an inexplicable feeling that I am interrupting him. This feeling is so constant that I can't shrug it off. But interrupting him from what?

Sometimes he loses track of what he later refers to as volume control. His anger turns to high at the tiniest thing: irritable would be too small and benign a word for this almost existential unease.

Things have changed, haven't they? They have changed completely and only a tiny bit. He seems in retreat, but from what?

The Tim that is left with me is a forgery. He moves through the world, functions more or less, but he is different.

One day, he throws something that smashes a vase on a cotton doily at his mother's house in the country. The flowered shards scatter. I go into the other room and say to Leo, who I am afraid may have heard something that might be disturbing to a seven-year-old, "Tim is a little grouchy."

"Tim is always grouchy," he observes. He doesn't look up from the graphic story he is writing, which seems to be called, "There is no comic." He is writing about a muffin who is a villain, and a marshmallow fleeing the police.

I settle next to him on the flowered couch. He looks up at me and says, "He'll calm down, don't worry."

I think about packing Leo and my things and leaving. Instead Leo and I take the dog for a long walk on the beach. Leo is wearing a neon orange hoodie; the rest of the beach is swallowed in fog, the horizon above the water a charcoal smudge. He runs ahead, a little neon spot.

A few weeks later, Tim falls next to one of the artworks he may or may not be selling and has something that looks like a very quick seizure on the floor. I think of calling an ambulance, but then he comes to, and insists it is nothing, and gets up and is fine. Violet is with me when this happens. We look at each other. He repeats, "It's nothing, I am fine." Somehow we go back to whatever we were doing before as if this is nothing and he is fine.

Reality defines itself around his words. It's like when he put AstroTurf on the living room floor to be Minecraft grass.

In one of the dark winter weeks, we finally make it out, alone, to a restaurant. But we have to leave right after the waiter pours water and puts down the menus. Tim is feeling violently sick. On the walk back through the warehouses, I tell myself that it's unfair to get angry with someone because they are sick, but it doesn't feel unfair.

For six months, eight months, I wonder: Is there something wrong with me and not him? I think: Is this just what marriage is, the other person slowly becoming a hologram of themselves, something you can see but never quite touch?

I live in a house where I could swear the dining room wall is cherry red, and then I walk into the room again and it's yellow. I can't tell you what color it really is. Probably orange. I am trying to live with this feeling, maneuver around it may be more accurate.

I tell him I have a weird feeling that I am pursuing him. He is angry that I am accusing him (though of what? I wonder. Of what?) I tell him it feels like something is wrong, and he says nothing is.

At times he is completely himself, warm, funny, etc., and at times completely not. It would be easier if he were never himself. The unevenness confuses me, the sometimes okayness of everything.

I stay up for hours at night, thinking about what the dark thing might be, wondering if the dark thing exists. Because it is unrealistic that Tim has been replaced by a different person out of a horror movie or surrealistic fairy tale, I am unable to truly take on board this theory, and yet I can't find another explanation for what is going on.

Eventually he tells me that the dark thing is Vicodin, and with effort the dark thing is banished.

While he recovers, I will worry about all the things that almost happened. I will worry about what the children have seen and what it will mean to them over time. I will not be angry at him because he is too destroyed. I will feel a rush of protectiveness, and by the time I can tell him I am angry, I won't be angry anymore.

I will, however, have time to think: *Now don't hang on my gun arm.*

The Saturday Meeting

The Al-Anon book: *It might be best to do and say nothing till things calm down.*

Holding back. Staying out of it. Remembering to do this in the heat of the moment.

Slowing down, because things are moving quickly. Words fly out, especially brutal ones, when something happens that scares or alarms you.

Not saying every single thing you are thinking about the situation.

I have to admit that this kind of restraint does not come naturally to me. I can't resist jumping in, offering my opinion. The program encourages silence, encourages waiting. *Does this need to be said? Does it need to be said by me? Does it need to be said by me now?* But I mourn all of the stupid little things I can't say.

Money

My mother on the phone: "It's kind of ironic that you married a rich person with no money."

The Wednesday Meeting

"In my house the truth was fungible," someone says. "The story in my family is that my mother died of a heart attack. That's what we say. But it is also very possible that she fell off the deck drunk."

There is something you know but don't know. There is the feeling of wondering if something is true, of going back and forth in your head, true, not true, true, not true, of doubting and second-guessing yourself until you are completely exhausted and wrung out and give up.

It is a relief to be in a room with people who know this feeling. I feel like I have been living alone on Mars, and suddenly I stumble across all these other people who are also living on Mars: they know the green lakes, the purple air.

Addicts often rearrange the facts, even when they are not doing drugs. The truth is shape shifting, it is what they need it to be in a given situation. They lie sometimes almost without knowing they are lying. What other people might think of as external reality is entirely subjugated to their continuing to do what they want to do and be who they are. They are stronger and more charismatic and more convincing than external reality. They have more charm. This can be disconcerting to live with.

In the rooms, I hear someone talk about "McDonald's liars." Someone who says that they are at McDonald's when they are at Burger King.

A pointless lie, a lie just for the sake of hiding, protecting, an instinctive, substanceless, almost recreational spinning of alternate truths.

Janet Malcolm: "We are all perpetually smoothing and rearranging reality to conform to our wishes; we lie to others and to ourselves constantly, unthinkingly. When, occasionally—and not by dint of our own efforts but under the pressure of external events—we are forced to see things as they are, we are like naked people in a storm. There are a few among us—psychoanalysts have encountered them—who are blessed or cursed with a strange imperviousness to the unpleasantness of self-knowledge. Their lies to themselves are so convincing that they are never unmasked."

In a past life, I used to love John Updike's line about most marriages being ruined by too *much* communication. And yet with Tim, I have basically become a truth obsessive. His lies, omissions, evasions, creative approaches to reality, about small things mostly, make me frantic. They spark an old fear of secret decay. A fear that the life we are living has some rot or corruption I can't see.

My fantasies of leaving Tim, which were, in a certain period, frequent and detailed, watching him carry his art down the stoop to a moving van, a parade of smoking handsome Israelis hoisting hastily wrapped furniture, are hollow. They are something I do sometimes to make myself feel better. *See, I could leave him.* But I can't. Or maybe I should say it in a less passive way: I won't.

Rebecca West:

"These women were keeping themselves apart from the higher purposes of life for an emotion that, schemed and planned for, was no better than the made excitement of drunkenness. One ought to pass into love reluctantly for life's sake, as one goes up into the mountains because he is very sick and to live longer on the plains means death."

Also: "I would waste on personal ends vitality that I should have conserved for my work."

Twitter

I stay up all night. I close my eyes and get into bed, but it's impossible to fall asleep. The feeling is of leaving a stove on that may burn down the house, only I haven't left the stove on. There are just a lot of people who would like my house to burn down.

I am not so arrogant as to think that my words on a page matter at all in the face of all this fantasizing. The angry fantasizing wins. Once a long time ago, at a reading, a woman opened a book of mine and pretended to read a passage about how women are asking for rape. The passage wasn't in my book. They were words I would never write. They expressed beliefs I would never hold. But she wore reading glasses.

"Katie Roiphe is the monster out of Stephen King's *IT*." "Retire, bitch." This goes on for days, weeks. The anger is always there and hard to avoid or forget about even when you are in pajamas packing school lunch for your child or putting the dogs out in the garden.

These strangers calling me "trash," "human scum," "a ghoul," "a garbage person," who write, "Suck my dick, Katie Roiphe," are angry about something they imagine might be in an essay I am writing in *Harper's* that hasn't yet come out. They threaten that I will never work again, which feels, given the ambient vitriol, like a definite possibility. Advertisers are pulling out of the magazine because of the anger. Will other publications want to take the risk of hiring me to write something?

The first night, a reporter calls to ask me for a comment. I do not have a comment.

One of these angry strangers, an editor at a respected men's magazine, made an oddly disturbing Halloween mask by punching out the eyes of a photograph of my face. Leo, maybe a little too adept at computers for an eight-year-old, comes across it. He asks, "Why would someone want to do that?"

A recurring fantasy: going out to coffee with a stranger who hates me. I picture someone with a job at *The New Yorker* or *The New Republic* and Elena Ferrante books on her bookshelf. Would it be hard to hate an actual person who smiled at you or seemed vulnerable, with dog hair on her sweater, say, or not that hard? What happens when there is an actual human confrontation with this vivid disembodied hate? The controversial classics professor at Cambridge Mary Beard entered into long email exchanges with Twitter haters, wrote job references for them, and beguiled and befriended them.

She is infinitely rational, infinitely understanding. She is everything under the sun but angry.

Mary Beard also posts a photo of herself crying after one of these intense Twitter furies with the caption "If you actually want to know, I am sitting here crying." This image is, of course, more powerful than the vicious phrases, the taunting.

I wouldn't have the courage to do that. I would never be able to post an image of myself crying. I am not sure I would even be able to cry. "I am fine. I am fine," I tell concerned friends on the phone. "These things blow over quickly." Of course, after Beard posts the crying photo, the Twitter mob perseveres: "White feminists weaponise the defense of innocence and insincere tears."

The article comes out. The chairman of my department explains to angry callers that the university doesn't fire people for their ideas. After a few days of it, though, the feeling is of being at war: the extra stuff—friendship, lunches, doctor's appointments, haircuts—falls away. Energy is conserved for the fight.

An editor at *Harper's* who doesn't like the piece posts a picture of an envelope with my home address, where I am living with the children, to the seven hundred followers on her Instagram with a spy emoji. She must think of this as a feminist act, making public the home address of a woman whose writing she doesn't like.

I obsess about the ideas in the piece. I email other people at three in the morning who are thinking about the ideas or adjacent ideas. I can't really talk to anyone who is not thinking about the ideas, who is not part of the war or doesn't care about it, which is most people.

In the midst of this, Tim peeks his head in the door to the room where I am working, if you can call what I am doing work, and brings up something I said to his ex-wife, whom I am on friendly terms with, that he doesn't think I should have said. "I can't talk about this right now," I say. "I'll rip your head off." I am joking, but I have been sleeping less than three hours a night for weeks.

"I'll rip your head off" is not something I would normally be able to say or even think or feel. Aggression is acceptable in this bizarre and temporary space. If there were a jury, it would say: self defense.

It's like I have absorbed all the hate into myself, converted it into power.

The Lord of the Rings

The therapist gives the nearly immediate impression of seeing right through both of us. She is terrifyingly smart. She deploys a kind of working crankiness shot through with humor: she has no patience for our various performances, which it's like she has seen before, lived with, gotten bored by, and is over. Occasionally she laughs at some bit of Tim outrageousness, but it's impossible to impress or obfuscate. This seems auspicious to us.

She points out that our most violent arguments are about what happened on a given night. We each desperately want the other to see and concede that our version is correct. We will pretty much fight to the death for this. We can't seem to learn that there is no point in litigating these moments. We were both there. We both know in our hearts that our version is the true one and the other person is lying or dangerously deluded. We both have to be right.

In this period Leo and I have been obsessively watching *The Hobbit* and *The Lord of the Rings*. The movies are essentially just one long flagrantly implausible yet weirdly exhilarating battle, elves against orcs, humans against goblins, dwarves against dragons, acts of insane physical bravura against a backdrop of unspeakable chaos. At some point I wonder: Why am I feeling the exact same thrill of identification and total transfixion as an eight-year-old boy? And then I realize that what I am recognizing is the desire to vanquish, the absolute recklessness and adrenaline of war. That's how I fight. Some warrior thing in me loves a battle. Sometimes winning can be more important to me than, say, being able to continue to live with the people I live with.

Of course, it's a cliché to say that everyone has their own side of a story, but the therapist's point goes farther than that. The idea is that each person literally experiences a different event. So even though you were both technically "there," you were having entirely different nights. Neither person is "right." Neither has or will ever obtain, as hard or ardently as they work for it, the power to persuade the other one. You are each living in a different marriage.

One power that is almost impossible to give up is the power of knowing what really happened. Letting the other person get away with their version. Letting it exist in the world. This is the hardest thing. Giving up the power over the story, the monopoly on truth. It feels impossible, what she is asking. Admitting that what I witnessed with my own eyes is only one thing that happened. On the other hand, it opens a window.

One day Tim says to her, "We've decided you should come live with us."

Graham Greene:

"The hurt is in the act of possession: we are too small in mind and body to possess another person without pride or to be possessed without humiliation."

Class

On Tuesdays, I teach a class called "The Art of Argument and Polemic." Some of my students struggle with the question of authority. I've come to believe that you have as much authority as you seize, but this is hard to put into practice. They want to know how you quiet the voice in your head, saying "Why should anyone listen to me?"

It is one of the hardest things to teach: confidence. The crazy reckless exuberant confidence most useful in polemic is even harder. We start by studying John Milton's Satan in *Paradise Lost*. How he persuades Eve to eat the apple even though she knows it is the one thing God says she can't do. Later I have them write against their deepest beliefs. I also have them write "Against" lists: "Against umbrellas," "Against Tinder," "Against talking about politics at dinner parties," against anything they want. All of this is to unloose them from their responsible, cautious selves. All of this is to trick the gods: Oh, it's not me, I am not the one picking this fight.

For me, authority, which is the form power takes on the page, is a fiction. It's not mine but something I dreamed up because I would like to have it.

I write my opinions as a fictional character, a me who is more certain, more flashy, more fearless, less polite, less concerned with approval, less afraid of risk. The actual me was so pathologically shy in kindergarten that several months into the year, the school had to call my parents and ask, "Does she talk?"

Oh, her, I seem to be saying, she sometimes goes too far.

When I began publishing polemics, Gloria Steinem attacked me. *The New Yorker* ran a long, painfully personal hatchet job that seemed to me to distort everything I had tried to do in my first book. It is hard to get across the humiliation of the public rebuke, the way it took over my mind, invaded every waking hour. At the beginning, it felt like it would be hard for things to get much worse. A pipe leaked into the closet in my decrepit one-room apartment on Jane Street and ruined most of my clothes. I felt some kind of shame, like I had done something beyond the pale, been caught at it, but then sort of like someone who finds a clean water source in a postapocalyptic landscape, freed and exhilarated. People can not like me, and I can survive. My whole world lit up with that feeling; it faded in and out, still fades in and out, but when I had access to it, it was incredible. An older male writer wrote to me calling the book a "barn burner." I liked the phrase. I was twenty-five. I was burning the barn.

More than ten years later, I was applying for my first real job. In a meeting of the entire journalism department, an older professor asked me if I still stood by the ideas in the book. I got the very distinct impression that she was asking me to renounce those ideas if I wanted her vote. She wanted me to recant. In the windowless room with twenty professors watching me or, I don't know, wondering what kind of sandwich to have for lunch, I felt that I was on trial for having these extreme thoughts.

I wanted the job so badly I considered backing off from that former self, brash, naive, very young. I saw a way I could stand there and be liked and be part of the club and be warmly approved of and taken in, in ways I never was. Everything I wanted I could have. But I couldn't do it. I said that I would have written the book differently now that I was older, I would have taken into account some of the more sophisticated rhetorical tools I was hoping to teach if I were hired, but I was still committed to the ideas in the book.

While I was writing the piece for *Harper's*, I asked myself a million times a day, why are you doing this? My life was finally so comfortable; I could go into the office and teach students I loved. I could write careful books that took years of research and inflamed nobody. Why would I go back into arguing against received ideas? Most of the time, the piece felt like crossing in front of moving cars. I stayed up for hours worrying about it. I had to talk myself into it every morning. And yet I couldn't walk away from it, either. The ideas I was trying to get across felt more important to me than peace of mind.

The impulse to say something most people don't want to hear may have less to do with bravery and more to do with desire. To be outside, to live in a little shack on the beach away from everyone else, to be exiled.

Deborah Levy: "Sometimes we want to unbelong as much as we want to belong."

I sometimes think about a spectacularly barbed comment Elizabeth Hardwick made about her very close friend Mary McCarthy: "There is something puritanical and perplexing in her lack of relaxation, her utter refusal to give an inch of the ground of her own opinion. She *cannot conform*, cannot often like what even her peers like. She is a very odd woman, perhaps oddest of all in this stirring sense of the importance of her own intellectual formulations. Very few women writers can resist the temptation of feminine sensibility; it is there to be used, as a crutch, and the reliance upon it is expected and generally admired." Her failure to conform. Her lack of relaxation. I can't get over the essentially scolding nature of this compliment.

Hardwick also talks about Mary McCarthy's "almost violent holding of special opinions."

The problem, Hardwick seems to suggest, is that there is something almost constitutionally wrong with her. *Odd* is the word Hardwick chooses for this wrong thing. She is standing out. She is not like us. The problem seems to be too much power, too conspicuous and showy and flamboyant a confidence. She dares to think her own "intellectual formulations" are important.

When my female students, the original ones, the ones who have something to say, are thinking to themselves, *Why should anyone listen to me?* they are responding in some deep way to this attitude which still floats in the ether. *Who are you to stand out?* They are responding to the implicit demand Hardwick is making: relax, conform.

(I don't like generalizing, but I have observed, male students who have something original to say seem overall less afflicted by these messages; they seem to find them easier to unlearn or override.)

Ultimately, Hardwick's reaction tells me less about Mary McCarthy than about the world that resists her, that has trouble tolerating her.

The smart women (and men) she is up against. The elaborate many-layered tiers of contempt. She was a bridesmaid in Hardwick's wedding. Hardwick published a vicious satire of one of McCarthy's most popular novels, *The Group*, under a pseudonym in the *New York Review of Books*.

Hardwick's exquisitely catty theory culminates in the idea that Mary McCarthy wanted attention but didn't care about being liked. This not caring is so hard to get at but also the greatest high. How do you get there? This is what I want to teach, what I want to learn.

Unlikable

Diana is the only person I show early versions of my writing to. I trust her opinions almost more than I trust my own. She has been my most important reader and editor for almost two decades. It is her I have in my mind when I sit down to write anything. She is the fixed point I am writing to.

When I am in a fog or losing confidence in a project, one lunch with her and I am restored. I have no idea how she does this. I just know that I get up from the table feeling re-focused and re-energized. I am not a hundred percent convinced that I can write anything without Diana.

I send her a few pages of the notebooks to see what she thinks. I warn her about how different they are from anything else I have ever written. A week later, I get an alarmingly tactful email suggesting we talk in person.

Diana and I meet in a bar in Midtown. She is the kind of person who gets right to the point. She says that "my character" is coming across as "unlikable." Or, as she struggles to make this sound a little better, "un-identifiable with."

"Why does she get out of the car?" She can't connect the me in the notebooks to the me she has had dinner with for almost twenty years, who seems funnier, healthier, fine.

She is struggling with how someone she likes or thinks of as at least normally assertive, and probably more so, could be so frustratingly, maddeningly abject.

When I don't admit enough weakness, I am unlikable. When I admit too much weakness, I am unlikable.

The thing that is most upsetting is that she so clearly wants very badly to like the pages. She just doesn't.

What's strange is that I understand completely. I know this frustration.

It is hard for Diana to pin down exactly what in the pages is unlikable; or rather the human situation prevents her from really trying. I am sitting in front of her, after all. I think part of the problem is that the "character," as we persist in calling her, is not forthcoming with feeling. She thinks and analyzes more than she feels. She is writing about a quite dark and unhappy scene, but she writes to understand rather than enact some sort of cathartic confession. The crying scene is still being withheld.

Because I see all of this quite clearly, one might very reasonably wonder why I can't fix it. If the unlikable woman can be liked, wouldn't she choose to? I love Diana and, more important, respect her as a reader on the highest plane; to ignore her is costly. In fact, it will cost me a summer of peace. I will wake up in the middle of the night for three months in a tiny house on an island, in Leo's grandmother's spare room, in a hotel room with Violet, and worry for hours about Diana not liking me (I mean "the character").

I am aware of a nearly immutable rule: If a man writes reasonably well about himself and his emotions as he moves through the world, he is innovating, admirable. A woman writing a thirty-page scene about looking for her child's shoe at a party would be a narcissist or crazy, but when Karl Ove Knausgård does it, Lorin Stein, then the editor of *The Paris Review*, says that "he has solved a big problem of the contemporary novel." By definition, for a woman to write about domestic life, however dysfunctional or dramatic, is small, and for a man it is large.

A woman writer writing about herself is basically guilty until proven innocent. We think, *Why can't she stop talking about herself?* Or we try to suppress this thought, but the effort of suppressing it spills into and corrupts our reading. When Diana says what I am writing is claustrophobic, would she say that about a male writer writing a roughly equivalent thing, or would his examination of his feelings about power have a sweeping scope, feel like green fields on a blazing day, have a kind of natural grandeur to it?

And yet it's not that what she is saying doesn't feel true to me. A woman talking about herself is claustrophobic, the effect is truly not enough air, my own effect is not enough air, I recognize that, but why is it not the same for a man?

We still see a woman who is not smiling in a photograph as "glaring" and the man as "thinking."

Diana gets stuck on the moment when I get out of the car with the baby. Why don't I just say no? She cannot make sense of the situation. It almost feels as if she is angry at "the character." She wants to shake her.

If only the character could just pull herself together! If she could explain these irrational, awkward, swirling moments or, better yet, avoid them entirely. Let's imagine her husband told her to get out of the car and she said, "No, I will not," and they drove home in tense silence, and she realized in a timely and orderly way that she should leave him. That would be preferable, would make more sense with everything else we know about her. If she could bring her considerable personal power to bear in the moments it really counts. If she could tell us in a more immediate way how she feels, instead of being so eerily detached, so cerebral and relentlessly critical. The reader wants to shout in frustration, "Are you ashamed? Are you sad?"

The real me, though. I could see only his anger. I could not process or perceive any other facts of the situation: the standard social contract requiring him to drive us home, the number of blocks away we are, the absence of a stroller.

For me it is like looking into a mirror and seeing a raw melting Lucian Freud painting instead of what you know or hope to be your face.

In the car, I have simplified myself, and folded myself up, into one thought: *How can I make him less angry?* In this case by getting out of the car so he can be alone. It is the family, I sense, that is impinging on him, driving him crazy. The only thing to do is to break the configuration.

A Russian doll: inside this idea is the idea that he never wanted a family. He thought he did because everyone does, but he didn't. I can make him less furious at this family that happened to him, that was inflicted on him, by disappearing.

Mary McCarthy wrote about "an alien personality" who was conjured in her marriage to Edmund Wilson, a her who was not her, who did things like light papers on fire and slip them under the door of his study, and this feels like an accurate way to put it. An alien personality (Martian, green-skinned, one-eyed) took the baby and walked home.

Later, when I walk into the house carrying the baby, he is friendly, friendlier than usual, as if nothing out of the ordinary has happened. I am relieved and respond the same way. I give the baby a bath, put her into her sky blue pajamas with cherries on them, read *My Many Colored Days* to her, put her in her crib with her purple blanket, sneak under my covers with a book.

Chris Kraus: "Why does everybody think that women are debasing themselves when we expose the conditions of our own debasement? Why do women always have to come off clean?"

Wednesday Meeting

I will not waste time trying to figure out the alcoholic.
Wanting to know why the alcoholic drinks, or when sober why he
does what he does, is an itch for which there is no scratch.

The idea that you can't know why someone drinks or does drugs and that you have to just live with the unknowable is radical for me. Not to try to figure it out, not to analyze, not to master the facts.

I do a lot of Google searches around drugs. Google "Opiates." Google "Suboxone." Google "Recovery."

Jamieson Webster in the *New York Review of Books*: "So what are painkillers, finally? They are drive-killers, which is why their effect on sexual function and even digestion is about the ceasing of work. This suggests the acute danger of these pills, insufficiently regulated, with drug companies profiting from this simple desire: no body, no drive, no pain, no helplessness, nothing. Stretched to the logical extreme, they are about permanent sleep. Death."

I tell myself that I am researching the problem, but I am looking for a specific answer to a specific question that is not on the internet: Why?

I'm coming to the idea that this isn't something you can know, that you have to leave someone alone with the mysteries of their personality.

In a letter to his brother, John Keats described negative capability as that state in which "a man is capable of being in uncertainties, Mysteries, doubts, without any irritable reaching after fact and reason." I have literally none of this. I am pretty much always irritably reaching after fact or reason. But paradoxically, having no idea what is going on and not trying to find out is weirdly empowering. Finding in yourself the ability not to know.

One danger of living with an addict: extremes and colorful happenings are in their own way alluring. In the addict's house you are never bored. You get used to an escalated life, to high dramas, even as you hate them and want to escape them. "I can't imagine wanting to kiss someone who wasn't an addict," a man says. "Or someone who wouldn't throw my heart under a taxi."

Another danger: the presence of the addict, even a sober addict, turns you into a brittle, vigilant version of yourself, that next to someone who might spin out of control, you manage, watch. I hate this drab part of myself, as much as or more than I fear the combustion in Tim or my sister. Who wants to be the boring person with the colorful person? The moralizing person with the wild one?

At Al-Anon the subtext is often power. The perverse ways that the less powerful in a family wield their own control. How the self-sacrificers exert their surprising stealth dominance. It asks you to reread your world. To stop trying for these tricky forms of power, or at least to be honest with yourself when you do.

Is it a luxury to be powerless? Think of a soldier who is on duty all night patrolling a perimeter, exhausted, terrified, alert. When he is relieved of this patrol, he can give up the watch and curl up in a warm sleeping bag. To give up the vigil. The night air cold and prickling with menace. To finally fall asleep in the tent. It feels like that.

Mary McCarthy

Simone de Beauvoir called Mary McCarthy a "cold and beautiful novelist who devoured three husbands and a crowd of lovers in the course of a neatly-managed career." This view of her fits nicely with her work and public image. But it doesn't fit with her life itself.

In her seven-year marriage to the critic Edmund Wilson, McCarthy does not seem to be devouring him. She says that he rolled her off the bed onto the floor because he didn't like the blue sheets she bought. He knocked her down in the kitchen and kicked her in the stomach while she was pregnant. He hit her in the face.

In a deposition on February 23, 1945, she states:

> Since the birth of our son I have tried to see this marriage through but from its inception to the present time I have been compelled to suffer physical and mental humiliation at the hands of the defendant. This has occurred in the presence of strangers, in the presence of friends, before our servants, the defendant's daughter by a former marriage and even before our son who is now 6 years old.

In a deposition on March 14, 1945, her friend Nathalie Rahv states:

> [He] appeared to take delight in scolding and upbraiding his wife for petty matters. He humiliated her in my presence and

in the presence of other friends by attempting to belittle her efforts at running the household and performing her wifely duties.

In a deposition on February 23, 1945, McCarthy states:

> Everybody had gone home and I was washing dishes. I asked if he would empty the garbage. He said, "Empty it yourself." I started carrying out two large cans of garbage. As I went though the screen door, he made an ironical bow, repeating, "Empty it yourself." I slapped him—not terribly hard—went out and emptied the cans, then went upstairs. He called me and I came down. He got from the sofa and took a terrible swing and hit me in the face and all over. He said: "You think you are unhappy with me. Well, I'll give you something to be unhappy about." I ran out of the house and jumped into my car.

He controlled all of their money, even the money she made from her writing. McCarthy said, "I had to ask him for a nickel to make a telephone call."

The day she met him, she wore a black dress and fox stole. He was a forty-two-year-old established literary critic. She was a twenty-five-year-old writer with green eyes, dark hair in a bun. She had three daiquiris before she met him because she was nervous and then two Manhattans with him and then passed out that night and woke up in a strange bedroom with no memory of how she had gotten there. She was not even remotely attracted to him, she reports, when she followed him into his study the next time she saw him, but she slept with him anyway.

Wilson also claims that she hit, bit, and scratched him like a cat. In his notebooks he called her "a hysteric of the classic kind." They both describe the incident where she pushed paper under his study door and set it on fire. After one of their early blowouts, he sent her to a mental hospital, where she stayed for twenty-one days. Her hand-written notes about the doctor's diagnosis say, "Without psychosis. Anxiety reaction."

They both drank a lot, and the only thing that they seem to agree on is that this drinking stokes the drama. In her "pincushion" letter breaking up with him, after a scene in Wellfleet, during which their son had "the wits scared out of him," she writes, "Up to the last ten days, I thought if I didn't have drinks anymore it might be better, but no."

He wrote to her from Wellfleet on *New Yorker* letterhead: "I feel terribly badly about all this, and I know that it was my fault that things got into such a mess."

It is difficult to imagine the Mary McCarthy of her books and essays ensnared in this situation for seven years. It is hard to imagine the famously ferocious writer suffering humiliation from anyone. *Time* called her "quite possibly the cleverest woman America has ever produced." She was famous for her terrifying fierceness at a time when almost no women writers were fierce. The critic Dwight Macdonald once said, "When most pretty girls smile at you, you feel terrific. When Mary smiles at you, you look to see if your fly is open." Randall Jarrell wrote a fictional version of her: "Torn animals were removed at sunset from that smile." It is strange to think of her legendary ferocity somehow vanishing or morphing in her marriage. This may be why she calls the person she was with Wilson "an alien personality."

Wilson wanted to groom or shape her as a writer. He thought their marriage would be *good* for her in a way that later irritated her. In her seventies, she writes about Philip Rahv, whom she was living with when she met Wilson: "His love, unlike Wilson's, was from the heart. He cared for what I was, not what I might evolve into. Whatever I might be *made* to be, with skillful encouragement, did not interest him. To say this today, may seem hard on Wilson, as well as ungrateful on my part for what he did to 'push' me into creativity. If he had not shut the door firmly onto the little room he shepherded me into. . . . I would not be the 'Mary McCarthy' you are reading today." He shut the door "firmly." He shepherded her. He "made" her into a creative writer. He "pushed" her. This language grates. She does seem to feel, however, that she needed his pushing to be the writer she became.

She likes to say that she wrote her first novel, *The Company She Keeps*, only because Wilson locked her in a room for hours. The fantasy that she put forward is that she is a prisoner, writing against her will almost; she is writing fiction because he is forcing her to. Something in this description always snags me. The hint of coercion, the giving over of will. She was by far the more brilliant sentence writer, some part of me protests, by far the more original and wide-ranging thinker. But maybe on this one thing she wanted someone to tell her what to do. It gave her the cover she needed to take the risk. She releases herself of responsibility, the risk is not purely hers. She is just doing what an older literary man told her to do.

Wilson wrote, "She had a childlike side that made one feel sorry for her."

He said he had "invariably wanted to rescue her."

About her domestic efforts, Wilson writes to her, "You have been wonderful except at those times when you turn the whole thing into a kind of masochism that is calculated to make other people as uncomfortable as you are."

Again it is hard to picture this kind of domestic masochism in someone as daunting as McCarthy. But for some reason she was determined to excel at domestic arts. She put her mind to them. She made two kinds of stuffing for Thanksgiving, oyster and chestnut. She didn't believe in labor-saving devices in the kitchen. It was as though all the competitive energy she had was also channeled into the creation of a home, into traditional femininity. She would not be outdone even in that.

Wilson writes to her, "I think, though, that as lovers, you and I scare and antagonize each other in a way that has been getting disastrous lately (though sometimes I have been happier and more exalted with you than I have been with anybody)."

In writing her memoirs, however, she becomes the cold and beautiful novelist of Simone de Beauvoir's fantasy, devouring husbands again, in command of her career. She reports coolly that she had never loved Wilson. One gets the sense she is writing over what happened. She is editing the relationship into something more tolerable, creating a self always in ironic distance, always powerful. She is mastering him in words.

The Thursday Meeting

One thing that bugs me in the rooms: having to be so understanding all the time. Sometimes I don't want to empathize with the addict or the angry man. It feels in these times like the program is trying to reason away your perfectly legitimate anger, while you desperately cling onto it, until you end up sheepishly giving it up.

"I am really trying to have compassion for him," someone says after describing a man it is very hard to have compassion for.

If a man is shouting at his wife, calling her a cunt in front of her seven-year-old son, why not just hate him? Life is short. I feel like I don't have time to muster any respect for the hidden intricacies of this man's psyche.

But I also get the idea that anger is panic. The angry man is lashing out because he is panicking, he is in extreme terror of something, he is threatened by forces he can't control. In the rooms, there is at least the faint possibility of compassion in this situation, of recognizing the angry man as someone whose systems are failing. It is probably no more fun to be the angry man than the woman he is thundering at.

Abusive

Tea with a newish friend I am very close to. One of those friendships where you meet and right away you think "I love you." She is
wearing an unusual, beautiful ring and some sort of platform clogs.
She had a childhood most people would not have survived in one
piece. When I try to understand what serenity might look like, I
think of her.

In passing, she matter-of-factly refers to her former husband as abusive. She is not making a point about their relationship, the story
is about something else entirely. It's a purely descriptive term she is
moving past.

I admire the ease with which she uses the word. The episode seems
closed in a good way, filed away.

I find the word difficult to use. In part because of its moral clarity, a
clarity I don't at all feel in relation to my own life.

I have always been uncomfortable with words that, in George Orwell's phrase, "think your thoughts for you." Jargony words. Politi-
cized words. This comes a little close.

At another point in my life I would probably have called a word like
this too "simple" for an incredibly intricate human situation, but it is

not simple. I would have called it "inadequate," which may be closer. But now I can see that it also has its uses. It might mark the point at which someone says, too much.

Now, of course, I love H. and see him all the time, uneventfully, innocuously, so it's awkward to give any words at all to that dark stretch. It's easier to think that a crazy thing happened between us a long time ago and that it is no one's fault. It's easier to think of it as a dream. He is so much a part of me and my entire adult life that I can't isolate him into a dramatic role. I like the blanched, washed-out version you tell a child: sometimes two people love each other but can't live together. I definitely prefer this way of looking at it to "abusive."

Other car rides: Leo asleep in the car seat, Violet singing along to the music, H.'s elbow out the window; H. showing up in the car to drive feverish baby Leo and me to the one pediatrician who is open very early on a Sunday morning; H. driving us to soccer to coach Violet's team; H. driving over from his house in a flood zone to spend the night during Hurricane Sandy because we are nervous.

If H. were telling the story of the car, if H. even *remembered* the story, what would his side of it be? Had I done something intolerable or said something awful while we were with our friends in their garden? Or could it just have been the claustrophobia of the family that descends on everyone once in a while but just a little more intensely. Like he had to be alone or he wouldn't be able to breathe. I can't blame him for this.

But the shouting? The neighbors calling the management company? The baby trembling so much she couldn't eat? From the outside it could look "abusive." It is true that he was loud and I was afraid.

To call him abusive is to admit his power over me. It feels like it is giving him power to say he abused it.

Even here in the notebooks I have already rewritten the story. I override my heart beating like a scared animal into "Not caring or not appearing to care is, in its own way, an assertion of power. Unruffled calm or even benumbed calm is its own kind of weapon."

It's not that this is wrong or untrue. But what I am avoiding or writing around or circling is my fear.

The word *abusive* strikes me as impossible, not just because of what it says about H. but because of what it says about me.

Torn-Out Pages

After visiting my mother, I lug home a tote bag of my notebooks from high school and college. ("Read me something pretentious," Tim begs.) One of them has a clump of pages near the back torn out. What happened in these pages?

I don't remember doing this, but in my novel I wrote a scene of a man tearing out pages of his notebook: "He took a straight razor out of the drawer and ran it down each offending page: it cut with pleasing violence, slicing through the tiny cottony threads, neat but somehow fleshlike. A surgeon of himself."

More Worrying

Tim is leaving on a work trip to Miami, and I am worrying that he is going to text while he is driving and crash the car and die. When I tell him this, he says, "I *have* realized that you can prop the phone up on the windshield and watch a movie while you drive."

Edge Play

Alexis starts as a random Facebook friend.

Bored one day, scrolling through a complete stranger's photos, I send her a message. Does she want to meet? This is something I have never done before or since.

The photographs were shot at the Chelsea Hotel. In one, she is standing on a velvet chaise longue in fishnet stockings and a corset, holding a whip above her head. Something intelligent, playful in the photos; she is referencing, conjuring.

Why did I do something so totally out of character? I make a date to meet her in a bar.

When she finally slides in next to me at the bar, she is one of her ordinary incarnations, jeans, Uggs, a black sweater. She drinks mint tea because she is sober. She reminds me of my sister Emily, and I feel instantly at home with her. My sister, who is not a dominatrix and tends to purposely lose power struggles so she doesn't have to be bothered with them. But they are somehow alike.

Her childhood: One day, when she was three, she was playing with a little boy and afterward his face was covered in scratches. She didn't have siblings so she learned to fight from cats. She grew up in a rent-controlled walk-up on the Upper East Side and wore a green-plaid uniform to school. She was the bohemian kid in a school full of girls with doormen.

Her years as a dominatrix: She was young in New York, a pretty, blond aspiring actress and artist, and felt from the men around her what she calls "microdismissiveness." She stumbled on a way to make money that also gave her instant power over successful older men. She worked in a dungeon for a while. She started freelancing with her own clients. She was drawn to the intensity, the boundary testing. "Edge play," they call it. She once participated in branding a man. She held the blowtorch, wearing a silver bikini and stilettos.

Subs. Slaves. Surgeons, finance guys, someone high up in the Department of Child Services who wants to be treated like an abused child, a Chinese billionaire who wants to be beaten bloody. A sub will come over and scrub her studio. Another pays for her to go out to an expensive dinner with her boyfriend and send him photos of their night together to humiliate him. I ask her if she ever thinks of finding a sub who will set her up in an apartment and support her, but she can't stomach that kind of dependence.

For as long as I have known her, Alexis has, in her own wily tactful way, been trying to explain to me that my idea of her as dominating is too simple. She moves between powerful and powerless; she is not fixed in one position. This is hard for me to understand since she is involved in such stagey, flamboyant, and fundamentally convincing exhibitions of power. I think of her as entranced with her own power. But her interest in the subject is more conflicted. She enjoys the feeling of power "when the cameras are rolling," as she puts it. But there is also a strong identification with the weak or exploited. Her obsession with power is as much about hating it as loving it.

When I met her, she was making highbrow fetish films for an eccentric individual collector who was bankrolling them. She kept blowing the budget because she would spend too much money on the aesthetics: the perfect vintage hospital bed from the twenties or a real goat skull for a Viking shoot. When I ask her why she seemed so much better in the films than the actresses she hired, she says, "I hit harder."

When she gets angry, you get a glimpse of the person who might not stop where she should. She is burning with it in a way I don't usually see women burn.

Some nights, things got out of hand. She punched a boyfriend once. She threatened another one with a whip, and he started running.

For most of the time I knew her, she was broke, living at home with her parents, burnt out on dominatrixing. She said to me once, "My dream is to run an exotic animal sanctuary." This kind of depressed me since it was so conspicuously one of those sad, impossible dreams a journalist would put in the story about a broke sex worker living with her parents as a nice ironic touch, and I wanted things to work out for her.

In our conversations neither of us could quite imagine her as a mother. She joked about how if she ever had a child, she would leave him outside making a snowman and find him later, frozen to death. She wanted to find a man who was like a housewife, a man with maternal instincts.

Then I blinked, and Alexis was running an exotic animal sanctuary in Indiana.

She has two emus, one camel, nine horses, three goats, two wolves, nine llamas, three alpacas, three rescue pigs, two inside dogs, two housecats, five feral cats. She also has a husband and two boys under two. This is one of my favorite developments of all time. She dominates even the universe into giving her what she wants.

She met a real estate lawyer at an AA meeting who helped her negotiate an improbable buyout for her parents' rent-controlled two-bedroom apartment on the Upper East Side, and she used that money, along with some money she'd scraped together herself, to buy a five-bedroom farm house in Michigan City, Indiana, on fourteen acres, abutting a huge nature preserve. She uprooted her whole life and moved, her mother along with her, to a totally new place in the middle of the country, hoping to figure out what to do there. In order to drum up an income, she went back to school to study addiction and family therapy and is starting a business called the Animal Connection, which uses animals to help recovering opiate addicts.

About both of us in the old days, she writes to me, "Maybe we felt a desire for power but we hated that we felt that way."

She met a man named Monty at a local farmer's market because he was selling emus, which are birds that look like "walking tiki huts."

They got married in her barn standing in the hay with the horse, goats, a ram in attendance. A silver tiara perched in platinum hair, a short white dress, knee-high caramel-colored boots, she has a Courtney Love vibe. Monty is tall, lanky, long-haired, handsome, and looks like a cowboy Jesus.

If I had ever pictured Alexis married, I would have thought of *Venus in Furs*, 1870: "In love there is union into a single being for a short time only . . . whichever of the two fails to subjugate will soon feel the feet of the other on his neck." But she was maybe done with that.

Monty had a half pit bull she felt was terrorizing her dogs. She wanted to get rid of the pit bull. He didn't want to get rid of the pit bull. They fought over this for a while, and then she realized this was not about the dog; it was about them mourning their autonomy. At times she felt forced "into a perpetual state of involuntary compromise."

This is hard for me to wrap my mind around: Alexis compromising, Alexis working things out.

The space helps. The horse pastures, the trees, the farmland, the stretch of nearby beach on Lake Michigan. She tells me about a Japanese therapy called "forest bathing."

She says, "Dominance gets boring, tedious." She quotes Virginia Woolf: "But to enjoy freedom . . . we have of course to control ourselves."

Monty names the camel "Camus" after his favorite writer. She rescues wild mustangs who are headed for the slaughterhouse. She gives birth to two babies, barely a year apart, at home on a covered porch.

She takes care of the finances, business decisions, plans. He builds additions to the barn, animal habitats. He is warm, peace-loving, patient.

For some reason, looking at a photo of Camus the camel makes me happy, or her toddler staggering naked through hydrangeas, or her fluffy white alpacas with Einstein hair in a purple basil patch, or a snowsuited baby peering at one of the wolves through a chain-link fence, or her mucking around the horses in rubber boots. This wild, implausible settling down.

This is what it comes to. Even your dominatrix friend has two babies, a husband, and makes her own cashew milk.

Simone de Beauvoir #4

If anyone can mine the allure of abjection while at the same time rising above it, it is Simone de Beauvoir.

She writes to Sartre, November 14, 1940, "Nothing in my life seems to count for me, except this need I have for you."

On September 25, 1939: "My heart is consumed by passion for you and it couldn't be more painful. This has been brewing all day, and it came down on me like a tornado in the streets of Douarnenenez, where I broke into sobs."

On December 12, 1940: "All that I can have of life without you I have—but it's nothing. I already knew that, when you were here—you are everything to me. I know it still better now, and find it both cruel and sweet."

On January 7, 1941: "I am wasting away with longing to see you. Do think about me."

On February 21, 1941: "I live but I'm mutilated. . . . I've dreamed hundreds of times that you are returning—I didn't go away for the Shrovetide holiday, so that I could wait for you. I scan every street corner for you. I live only for the moment when I set eyes on you again."

They spent large swaths of time apart; often he was with another woman. One gets the feeling in the letters that she is taking pleasure, almost reveling in, the abjection, not just that she is missing their relationship but that this missing *is* their relationship, this hunger is itself almost a creative production: "Our affair," she writes to him, "seems as moving to me as a beautiful novel."

Her long-maintained abjection is almost an achievement, the sustained intense need. In certain lights, suffering for love becomes living fully. Chris Kraus writes that you can turn abjection into something "bright and exalted like presence." This seems like an idea that de Beauvoir would agree with. Interestingly, it seems like Sartre would also agree. He says that unlike his love, hers "is really a *thing* and a thing that is present, it has no face but is like a weight."

This abjection is both ultrafeminine, in its traditional expression of need for a man, in being nothing without him, in its expression of utter dependence, but also daring, in its assertion of desire, or maybe too much desire, excessive or unmanageable or sometimes even unwelcome desire. When de Beauvoir says her relationship with Sartre is her greatest accomplishment, it is a taunt and maybe also her true belief.

I am not suggesting this feeling she describes is not real, is counterfeit or performed, but that the importance of writing it is there, too. That it is her creation. She claims it for her own.

They are often apart for many months, so much of their relationship takes place in letters, it is in the sentences. Sartre's letters are also full of declarations of devotion, but they are less panicked, less voracious, less passionate, more tender. ("I'd so like to see your good little face.") His letters are suffused with affection; they are fond and calm. He does not cultivate or whip up desperation. He continually talks about how he wants her to be happy. He likes to think of her happy. He is not trying to provoke a frenzied or pining or suffering love. ("It horrifies me a bit to think you have suffered from our separation and that you're still unhappy from it.") He is not offering her suffering the way she is offering it to him. He says about his love, "I don't know how to make you feel it."

His letters are also constrained by his other affairs. He writes to de Beauvoir with a lover sitting across from him at the table and worries about her reading upside down. He tears up de Beauvoir's letters because this lover may read them, even the ones de Beauvoir has specifically asked him to keep.

Sometimes I can't stand the letters to Sartre. I have to put them down, take a walk. This type of female vulnerability, especially in someone I admire, is deranging. How can she? And yet it seems undeniable that de Beauvoir's interest in abjection, her life's experiment in it, is under her control. *I am mutilated. As beautiful as a novel.*

A boyfriend once divided the world into two kinds of people, "the haunters" and "the haunted." If this were true, de Beauvoir would be "the haunted." At the time he said this, I thought I would always want to be "the haunter." That sounded like the more powerful position; it's pure power, almost the definition.

Only later did I understand that being "the haunted" is the true high; only later still, that seeing the world in this way at all is dangerous.

In de Beauvoir's strange extended interview with Sartre toward the end of his life, which takes place mostly in Rome, they talk about sex.

> SIMONE DE BEAUVOIR: In your case it was only the active side that was developed. That led you to self-control, but at the same time to a certain coldness.
>
> SARTRE: Almost to a slight touch of sadism. Since in the end the other person was yielded up, and I was not.

Over and over she refuses the narrative of abjection, of being exploited or taken advantage of, yet she freely acknowledges her position, her dependence on him, her desperation. She accepts that their relationship is in some ways lopsided, that their immense need for each other is different. She accepts "a certain coldness."

In the section of *The Second Sex* devoted to "The Independent Woman," she writes, "For a woman to accomplish her femininity she is required to be object and prey; that is, she must renounce her claims as a sovereign subject. This is the conflict that singularly characterizes the situation of the emancipated woman. She refused to confine herself to her role as female because she does not want to mutilate herself; but it would also be a mutilation to repudiate her sex."

In one of his letters to her Sartre refers to her "frail little iron willed self." The power of these contradictions is irresistible. *Iron willed. Frail.* The perfect appeal of being both.

When *The Second Sex* came out, Elizabeth Hardwick wrote about the book's "brilliant confusion." The inspired refusal to resolve.

Chris Kraus: "He asked me why I made myself so vulnerable. Was I a masochist? I told him, 'No. "Cause don't you see? Everything that's happened here to me has happened only 'cause I've willed it.'"

Mother #2

My mother has neck surgery because she is losing her balance. The surgery is a success, but the immediate aftermath is worse than we expected, the pain fierce, unmanageable.

When she gets home from the hospital, she lies propped up on four pillows. She can't stand or walk without help. She is wearing some sort of pink Indian cotton pants I have never seen before. She lets me rub moisturizer, which she hates, on her hands and feet, probably because she is taking Valium every three hours and Percocet every four hours. She is flying, though not in a good way.

She hates drugs. She hates the feeling of being groggy or out of it. She has elaborate moral feelings about opiates, too. She knows that heroin was not the root cause of my sister's difficulties, but she blames it with a deep personal animus, as if the drug has broken into her home late at night and stolen something from her.

The pain comes in waves, even with the painkillers. She doesn't like air-conditioning, so the room is tropical. She mostly stares and naps and pretends to read the *New York Times*. The paper strewn on her bed, the reading glasses, are reassuring, traces of her old self. If you ask her how she is, she is angry.

In regular life, she has tons of friends, lunch dates, dinners, coffees, romantic friendships, flirtations, parties, book clubs, Torah groups, museum visits, but none of this helps now. When I ask her if she wants to speak to a friend, she looks at me as if I have just suggested that she might want to go waterskiing.

We stare at each other. The staring seems to be leading us in no good direction. I try to interest her in politics. I try mindless chatter about the kids, but her sharpness is gone with the painkillers. Nothing catches her interest. She is swimming toward what I am saying through a deep sea.

I say, "Oh, I forgot to tell you. I went to see Leo's play. He was the sportscaster in a race between a cheetah and a sloth."

"It's harder for boys than for girls."

"Sometimes, yeah."

"But I am glad he is getting what he wanted out of it."

Something seems to be altering, some chemical is blooming. Suddenly she is less miserable, maybe even a little sociable.

"I like your tiger mane," she says. "I mean lion's mane."

"Well, thanks."

"Did you get the tickets?"

"Tickets to what?"

"You know, the tickets for the Last Meal."

"Oh, yeah. I got them."

"Oh, good."

She closes her eyes. I wonder if she is falling asleep.

Her eyes are closed. "You know, this restaurant is very pretty, but it leaves something to be desired in terms of health."

"It sure does."

She is perched alone up there on her Valium mountain.

Later, she tells me exactly which window of her apartment she will jump out of if her walking doesn't get better.

We are leafing through a box of photographs that articulate the problem with almost too much clarity. She is living alone in her eighties, at the time in her life when she most needs someone to take care of her. She is without my father, who made coffee for her every morning, who cooked every dinner for her, who calmed her with his quiet. She would rather be in a different part of her life, sunkissed, blue jean jacket, mass of curly hair blowing, on the beach with my father, curly-haired moppets running in the dunes with the dogs. We would be eating a picnic of Nantucket sandwiches, which were thick slices of tomato, red onion, mayonnaise on white bread my father baked, in another paper bag grapes with a little sand in them but no one cared. We come across a photo of her reading to us, one of those days, on a towel. She would like to go back to that day. It's frustrating not to be able to get there. There is nothing I can do but sit next to her on the bed. At least I bought the tickets to the last meal.

Air-conditioning

That evening I walk to the subway past the bodegas with flowers in plastic pails. A line from *To the Lighthouse*: "We perished, each alone."

I want some proof that this is not true, some physical collision with evidence to the contrary. But when Tim gets home at night, he is angry that I have turned off the air conditioners. He likes to leave them on for hours when he leaves the house, he likes frosty, low-grade winter all the time, but I always turn them off when no one is around, and now he is just ranting about the air conditioners, and so I lie on a thin strip of bed, as far as I can from him, reading a novel someone sent me about a house cleaner who falls in love with a heroin addict. Is this what marriage is, one person worrying about the state of the air-conditioning and the other one thinking "We perished, each alone"?

The Doctor

I am having lunch with a new friend in Marylebone, her rooftop terrace overlooking an ancient church tower somehow sunny and exotic, fig trees, lemon trees, hibiscus. She is eighty-five, immensely tanned, bright blue eyes, wearing an Indianish kaftan, a presence. She is a doctor, became a very successful one in the days before women became doctors; she is rigorous, outrageous, relentlessly original, her Boston terrier napping beneath the wrought-iron table.

We peel eggs and eat chicken. The wasps hover. The sun is intense, the sky a startlingly clear blue for London. We have somehow launched right into the most intimate pressing subjects. She is no-nonsense and is for some reason specially interested in and attuned to issues of power. Her own marriage was enormously complicated and unconventional. Pretty soon she has me telling her my entire romantic history, she is somehow extracting it from me like a medical history. She is actually taking notes. I find myself wanting to impress her, but I am trying to be accurate.

There is something confusing about you, she says. These men who come in and out, but you don't care. They are not affecting you.

Somewhere in the process of turning my romantic history into a story, I have drained it of any signs of my being crushed. I have taken out any heat. I have elaborately narrated being powerless without somehow showing any powerlessness.

I have hidden the abject feeling, where it comes up, concealed it in funny or outlandish details. I tell her about the Claw's girlfriend calling me out of the blue. But it is a funny story, a curio. It is so drained of feeling that even I have trouble remembering if at the time I did care. Even calling the Claw "the Claw" is, of course, a way of flattening him into a cartoon, of denying and turning to parody the painful human attachment.

I tell her the car story, but the me who leaves the car is not terrified that her husband will leave. She does not get out of the car hoping to pacify and hold on to him, to get him to stay with her. She has somehow turned into an interesting collector of difficult men, an adventurer. The facts glimmer, as if the light is changing. The tone is blithe, the self I am putting forward is unscathed, untouched.

When my new friend was young, she walked across the grass at medical school overhearing male students saying disparaging things about her. I don't think I would have been able to do that.

But this is wrong. I want to convey to her the real tenor. I want to get it right to her in particular. This somehow becomes important. I have a feeling there is something she can teach me or explain for me but only if I can get the truth of my experience across. I want to get at the abjection in the story, the pain or difficulty that I have somehow almost sought out. There is so much of it, but I find I can't. She is making ginger tea. We are talking about Bloomsbury people her mother knew. The moment passes.

I glance at my phone. Somehow more than four hours have passed. I've been there for so long, there is a text from Tim: "I forgot what you look like."

The Car

The other day H. mentioned that he had bought the blue car because I'd seen it on the street with a FOR SALE sign in the window and told him I liked it. I was startled because I hadn't remembered until he said it. But it's true! He bought the car for me.

Sylvia Plath

"I am aware of a cowardice in myself, a wanting to give up. If I could study, read, enjoy people on my own, Ted's leaving would be hard, but manageable."

"How can I live without him? I mean if I could write & garden & be happy with my babies, I could survive. But I am so sick & sleepless & jumpy all is a mess."

In the years before he leaves her, the letters obsess over her dream of a perfect, artistic domesticity, how tantalizingly close she is to it. When you send me two pairs of tights, when we paint the floors, when we borrow a proper heater, when you send me Toll House chocolate morsels because they don't have them here, when we sell a few more poems, when I get a sewing machine, when we get a house in the country, when we get a flat in London.

He looms over all of this, brilliant, virile, dangerous. The sexual happiness. The only man she cannot boss. He takes her steak and mushrooms and a glass of red wine in bed when she is recovering from the strain of her exams.

The letters she writes to her American psychiatrist shock me. It is early July 1962. She has just discovered for a hard fact that Ted is cheating on her with an exotic-looking woman who works in an advertising agency and has rented their flat in Primrose Hill.

In these first crazed letters to the psychiatrist, she is trying to solve the problem of herself. How can she change to accommodate him? The moment of trying to hold on to this consuming love, before she sees that it is over. The letters are darting, distressed, wild.

"How can I make these women unnecessary to him? And keep up my own sense of seductiveness and womanly power? I don't want to be sorrowful or bitter, men hate that, but what can I do in the face of these prospects?"

"Can you suggest a gracious procedure when you see some little (whoops, not little, big!) tart is after your husband at a party, or dinner or something? Do you leave them to it? Engage a hotel room? Smile & vanish? Smile & stand by? What I don't want to be is stern & disapproving or teary. But I am only human. I have to feel I have some ground-rights."

"I am, by the way, not fat!!"

This feels familiar, also repellent. How can I solve the problem of myself so he wants to stay?

She writes, "Other men seem ants compared with him. I am physically attracted to no one else. All the complexities of my soul & mind are involved inextricably with him."

"I was prepared for almost anything—his having the odd affair, travelling, drinking (I mean getting drunk)—if we could be straight, good friends, share all the intellectual life that has been meat and drink for me, for he is a genius, a great man, a great writer."

I am tempted to throw the book at a wall. The elaborate accommodating. The clinging to any small part of him. Plath's famous cold fury is more palatable. "Out of the ash/I rise with my red hair/and I eat men like air." But this other Plath, trying to hash things out with the psychiatrist, trying to understand, trying to work things out, to compromise, to find solutions, to understand a genius, to keep a man, is there, too.

Her American psychiatrist writes to her, "First, middle and last, do not give up your personal one-ness. Do not imagine that your whole being hangs on this one man."

The letters make it clear that Plath pretty quickly experienced Hughes's departure as creative force. She saw very clearly that the poems she was writing after he left that fall were by far her strongest, that something wild and original had been shaken loose in her. She ate very little. She took sleeping pills at night. She wrote at five a.m. before the babies woke up. But that wasn't enough. The poems weren't enough.

She offers to pay the doctor to write back to her letters. The doctor refuses the payment but writes to her anyway: "*Do not imagine that your whole being hangs on this one man.*"

The sad thing to watch is that she was trying to make her way to the doctor's words. "The part about keeping my personal one-ness is a real help. I must. But my god I can't see to thinking straight." Four months later, she was dead.

Island-ess

I am reading Plath's anguished last letters. Tim is cooking.

We are on an island, no cars, only boardwalks, beach, grass. I like that there is not much to take in here; the colors are only the gray of beach-worn wood, green, blue, sand. There is one grocery store we walk to, but other than that there is nowhere to go but the beach.

The walls of the small square house are glass doors, which we leave open, so you can see right through the main room, which opens onto decks in the front and back.

Tim is cutting onions, carrots, celery. He is precise and patient, pushing tiny squares of vegetables from the cutting board into a bowl with the side of the knife. He is careful when he is cooking, even though he is careful in no other area of life.

Plath: "I am bloody, raw, nerves hanging out all over the place, because I have had six stormy but wonderful years, bringing both of us, from nothing, books, fame, money, lovely babies, wonderful loving, but I see now that the man I loved as father and husband is just dead."

Plath: "Then the terrible evenings settle in. The shock of this has almost killed my heart. I still love Ted, the old Ted, with everything in me & the knowledge that I am ugly and hateful to him now kills me."

Tim stirs the sauce with a wooden spoon, ducks to check something in the oven.

Plath: "She is so beautiful and I feel so haggish & my hair a mess & my nose huge, & my brain brainwashed & God knows how I shall keep together."

In the months after she first met Hughes, Plath wrote a poem called "Spinster" in which she described living alone: "the heart's frosty discipline exact as a snowflake."

Tim is assembling a salad for the rest of us. He doesn't eat salad.

Plath writes, "I lost myself in Ted, instead of finding myself."

You can see the pinkness over the water through the lattice of branches. Streaks of fire orange. Tim is laying out forks, putting down plates, red napkins, a bottle of wine, on the picnic table. I watch him, white linen shirt, his face showing the sun.

One of my sisters used to say, thinking of my calamitous taste in men, "Maybe one day you will make a good choice by accident."

The kids are still bobbing in the pool with two of my former students, who are visiting. They are playing an intensely competitive game that involves diving for small stones. The smaller dog perches uneasily on the edge watching them, torn between his extreme clinginess to humans and his terror of water.

Chris Kraus writes in the last letter to Dick, "No woman is an island-ess."

The deck is still warm, beach grass scraggling through wood planks.

CODA

One morning I woke up and didn't get out of bed. I no longer felt like writing in the notebooks. Nothing was calling me to them.

The smaller dog trekked up my side like a mountain climber and stood there on my shoulder for a minute, trying to ascertain if I was going to get out of bed to feed him, which I wasn't.

Of course the project is unfinished, can never be finished. How to balance clashing feelings toward power without being totally exhausted. How to live in shifting sands. Also: how to go on being a writer without certainty.

To be so exposed feels dangerous, but having done it, I also feel free. In Al-Anon they say, "You are only as sick as your secrets."

A friend of mine owns the photograph of Simone de Beauvoir in her forties, standing naked in a bathroom in heels. She hung it in the hallway outside her bathroom. I imagine her passing it every day in a robe.

The idea of just living with yourself, of tolerating the contradictions, incongruences, of letting things lie.

A few days ago, I read a passage by the Italian writer Natalia Ginzburg that seemed to zero in on my situation with Tim: "The strange thing is that we always feel so good, so at peace with him; we can breathe freely; our brow, for years so furrowed and sullen, suddenly relaxes; we never tire of talking and listening. We realize we've never had a relationship like this with any human being; all human beings, after a while, come to seem quite harmless, simple and small. Walking beside us at his own distinct pace, with his austere profile, this person possesses an infinite power over us: he can do us any kind of good or harm. And yet we feel a boundless tranquility. And we leave our home and go to live with him forever."

In the bed, Tim is asleep in the button-down shirt he wore yesterday. He sleeps in his day clothes and wears white cotton pajama pants outside, which I guess makes sense since there is really no inside and outside for him.

Outside, bare treetops etched against dark sky, the blur of streetlamp. The dog settling back into blankets.

More Ginzburg: "Sometimes violent conflicts erupt between us, yet they cannot destroy that boundless inner peace. And only years later, many years later, after a dense web of habits and memories and violent conflicts has been woven between us, do we finally know that he truly was the right person, and we couldn't have lived with anyone else; only in him could we seek all our heart requires."

This dark room. Not wanting anything to change. I close my eyes and go back to sleep.

A partial list of books I used, quoted, referred to, thought about, was influenced by, or obsessed with while writing the notebooks:

Women & Power, Mary Beard
I Love Dick, Chris Kraus
Outline, Rachel Cusk
Crudo, Olivia Laing
One Day at a Time in Al-Anon, Al-Anon Family Groups
Speedboat, Renata Adler
The Argonauts, Maggie Nelson
Mrs. Bridge, Evan S. Connell
The Folded Clock: A Diary, Heidi Julavits
Why Did I Ever, Mary Robison
Cast a Cold Eye, Mary McCarthy
Intellectual Memoirs, Mary McCarthy
Difficult Women, David Plante
The Golden Notebook, Doris Lessing
Journal of a Solitude, May Sarton
Life with Picasso, Françoise Gilot and Carlton Lake
The Silent Woman, Janet Malcolm
The Journalist and the Murderer, Janet Malcolm
*Words in Air: The Complete Correspondence Between Elizabeth Bishop
    and Robert Lowell*, edited by Thomas Travisano with Saskia
    Hamilton

Tête-à-Tête: The Tumultuous Lives and Loves of Simone de Beauvoir and Jean-Paul Sartre, Hazel Rowley

The Woman Destroyed, Simone de Beauvoir

The Second Sex, Simone de Beauvoir

The Mandarins, Simone de Beauvoir

Adieux: A Farewell to Sartre, Simone de Beauvoir

James Baldwin: Collected Essays, edited by Toni Morrison

The Lonely City: Adventures in the Art of Being Alone, Olivia Laing

A Room of One's Own, Virginia Woolf

Are You My Mother?, Alison Bechdel

A Bolt from the Blue and Other Essays, Mary McCarthy

Feel Free, Zadie Smith

The Empathy Exams, Leslie Jamison

The Recovering: Intoxication and Its Aftermath, Leslie Jamison

Slouching Towards Bethlehem, Joan Didion

Reborn: Journals and Notebooks, 1947–1963, Susan Sontag, edited by David Rieff

What Happened, Hillary Rodham Clinton

Simone de Beauvoir: A Biography, Deirdre Bair

Wuthering Heights, Emily Brontë

Sexual Politics, Kate Millett

A Lover's Discourse: Fragments, Roland Barthes

The Letters of Sylvia Plath, vol. 2, edited by Peter K. Steinberg and Karen V. Kukil

Alice's Adventures in Wonderland, Lewis Carroll

Good Morning, Midnight, Jean Rhys

The Collected Poems of Sylvia Plath, edited by Ted Hughes

The Collected Essays of Elizabeth Hardwick, edited by Darryl Pinckney

In Love, Alfred Hayes

The House of Mirth, Edith Wharton

Edith Wharton: A Biography, R.W. B. Lewis

Edith Wharton, Hermione Lee

The Letters of Edith Wharton, edited by R.W. B. Lewis and Nancy Lewis

The Age of Innocence, Edith Wharton

Jean Rhys: Life and Work, Carole Angier

The Lonely Crowd, David Riesman

Voyage in the Dark, Jean Rhys

Quartet, Jean Rhys

The Spy Who Loved Me, Ian Fleming

The Judge, Rebecca West

The Fountain Overflows, Rebecca West

In the Freud Archives, Janet Malcolm

The Quiet American, Graham Greene

The Cost of Living, Deborah Levy

My Struggle, Karl Ove Knausgård

The Company She Keeps, Mary McCarthy

Seeing Mary Plain: A Life of Mary McCarthy, Frances Kiernan

Mary McCarthy: A Life, Carol Gelderman

Writing Dangerously: Mary McCarthy and Her World, Carol Brightman

The Letters of John Keats, edited by H. Buxton Forman

America Day by Day, Simone de Beauvoir

A Collection of Essays, George Orwell

Venus in Furs, Leopold von Sacher-Masoch

Witness to My Life: The Letters of Jean-Paul Sartre to Simone de Beauvoir, 1926–1939, ed. Simone de Beauvoir

Letters to Sartre, Simone de Beauvoir, edited by Quintin Hoare

To The Lighthouse, Virginia Woolf

The Little Virtues, Natalia Ginzburg

A Place to Live: And Other Selected Essays of Natalia Ginzburg, Natalia Ginzburg